To
the memory of

Muriel Lester

traveling secretary of the
International Fellowship of Reconciliation,
who introduced me to the life and thought
of Mahatma Gandhi

"Generations to come will scarce believe that such a one as this ever in flesh and blood walked upon this earth."

Albert Einstein

"If humanity is to progress, Gandhi is inescapable. He lived, thought, and acted, inspired by the vision of humanity evolving toward a world of peace and harmony. We may ignore him at our own risk."

Martin Luther King, Jr.

Mahatma Gandhi

Nonviolent Liberator

MAHATMA GANDHI

Nonviolent Liberator
A Biography

Richard Deats

New City Press
Hyde Park, NY

Published in the United States by New City Press
202 Cardinal Rd., Hyde Park, NY 12538
www.newcitypress.com
©2005 Richard Deats

Cover design by Miguel Tejerina
Cover photo: a portrait of Gandhi given to Kingsley Hall in London in 1953 by
the government of India in rememberance of Gandhi's stay there in 1931.
Photo taken by Rich Wilken

Excerpts from Mohandas Gandhi's writings are used with kind permission from
Navajivan Trust, Ahmedabad-380 014, India

Printed in the United States of Amierca

Contents

Foreword

When I joined the Fellowship of Reconciliation in 1974, I found in staff member Richard Deats a role model and friend within the growing community of those seeking to understand nonviolence more deeply and to pursue it as a form of social action. Through public witness on the side of justice and peace, workshops, lectures, writings, and creative work as editor of *Fellowship*, Richard Deats has made a major contribution to a growing understanding of nonviolence as a realistic way of constructive social change. He has taught Gandhian nonviolence far beyond the shores of the United States. For many of us he embodies the spirit and teaching of Gandhi and Gandhi's relevance for our times.

Drawing upon his long study of Gandhi and upon his relationships with many who knew Gandhi personally, Deats has written *Mahatma Gandhi: Nonviolent Liberator*, a lucid account of Gandhi's life and work to free India from colonial rule. Deats skillfully connects Gandhi's community-building on the local level with his national campaigns of nonviolent civil disobedience against injustices of the British regime. For those who know little or nothing about him, this book provides an introduction. Those already familiar with Gandhi will find a trove of excerpts from the large corpus of the Mahatma's writings.

Deats correctly sees Gandhi first and foremost as a seeker of God, and consequently as a nonviolent liberator whose actions flowed directly from his search for truth, a search nourished by a consistent practice of prayer. Gandhi's own words demonstrate how he came to see truth as identical with love — not love as a sentiment, but love as the effective willing of the true good of all, and the clearest and deepest human experience of God. This clarity of belief translated into action, action that involved bearing suffering while refusing to inflict it on others, gave Gandhi his great and abiding influence. He demonstrated that power arising from acts of love is infinitely more potent than power obtained by violent force.

This book will help many understand nonviolence as a realistic alternative to violence as a political instrument. Today, violence threatens all creation in ways we dare not ignore. Gandhi saw this with a clarity that still eludes many policy makers. His response to the two atomic bombings of 1945 conveys the urgency he felt. He wrote, "So far as I can see, the atomic bomb has deadened the finest feeling that has sustained humanity for ages. . . . Humanity has to get rid of violence only through nonviolence. Hatred can be overcome only by love."

Gandhi's lifelong experiment with active nonviolence is his legacy to us. His life and teaching have influenced the civil rights movement in the United States as well as nonviolent transfers of power in a number of other countries. His life and words demonstrate the power of love and truth as a response to the violence of dehumanizing poverty and political oppression. We owe Richard Deats our thanks for a book that will build and extend Gandhi's influence.

Mary Evelyn Jegen, S.N.D.

Mary Evelyn Jegen, a founding member of Global Peace Services U.S.A., is an author, lecturer, and former vice president of Pax Christi International.

Preface

My life has been profoundly shaped by three mentors —
Muriel Lester, Martin Luther King, Jr., and Mohandas
Gandhi. Lester and King I knew personally; both of them
were deeply indebted to Gandhi for his spirituality and for
his philosophy of nonviolence, and through them I was led
to Gandhi's vast writings and his work in South Africa and
India.

Similarly, Gandhi influenced many of my early teachers
and friends — Howard Thurman, Amiya Chakravarty,
E. Stanley Jones, Dorothy Nyland, J. Waskom Pickett,
K. K. Chandy, Hildegard Goss-Mayr, and Jim Lawson.

During the thirteen years I lived in Asia, I traveled exten-
sively in India and was able to visit some of the places associated with Gandhi and the Freedom Movement of the
subcontinent — Calcutta, Bombay, Delhi, Madras, Kerala,
Shantiniketan. I was at the Birla Mansion in Delhi (where
Gandhi was assassinated) during the filming of Richard
Attenborough's magnificent "Gandhi." I made a pilgrimage
to the Rajghat in Delhi, the memorial stone where the last
rites of the Mahatma were performed on January 31, 1948.
I attended the Triennial Meeting of the International

Fellowship of Reconciliation (IFOR) in 1981 held at the Christavashram in South India, headquarters of the India Fellowship of Reconciliation. The India FOR was founded in 1950 by K. K Chandy during a visit to India by Muriel Lester, traveling secretary of the IFOR. K. K. Chandy, for many years secretary of the India FOR, was a friend of Gandhi and others active in India's nonviolent freedom struggle.

In my peace ministry spanning the last half of the twentieth century, I have continued to drink deeply from the well of Gandhi's life and thought. As I have lectured and led workshops in nonviolence around the world, I have found Gandhi's influence profound wherever people are struggling for deliverance from injustice and oppression. In South Korea, during the Park dictatorship in 1977, while leading underground workshops I met with the Korean Gandhi, Ham Sok Hon. When I was part of the IFOR's nine weeks of nonviolence workshops in the Philippines in 1985 during the dictatorship of Ferdinand Marcos, Filipinos were especially receptive to Gandhi's message because the leading opponent of Marcos, the imprisoned Senator Benigno Aquino, had had a deep conversion in his cell while reading the Bible and the writings of Gandhi. He came to advocate the necessity of a nonviolent revolution in the Philippines. Although subsequently assassinated, the Filipinos picked up his banner as they brought about a nonviolent, "people power" revolution in their country in 1986. In Soviet Lithuania in 1990, as that first breakaway republic in the USSR prepared for independence in the face of Soviet tanks, Lithuanian TV broadcast the movie "Gandhi" every night. The next year I organized a group of nonviolence trainers to go to newly independent Lithuania to assist the nonviolent resistance there to continued Soviet control.

Gandhi's influence was brought home to me in an unexpected way in 2001 on the tenth anniversary of the sanctions on Iraq, which had contributed to the deaths of hundreds of thousands of Iraqis. I joined in a liturgy and vigil on the steps of the US Mission to the United Nations in New York City. We asked the US Ambassador to join us in a typical Iraqi meal, a meager ration of lentils and rice and unfiltered water. The Ambassador did not come out. Instead sixteen of us — nuns, priests, ministers, persons of various religious traditions — were arrested for trespass, handcuffed and taken eventually to the infamous "Tombs" at 100 Center Street in Manhattan. We were led in chains, fingerprinted, and placed in group cells until the next afternoon, when, after facing a judge, we were released.

During the sleepless night I prayed for the children of Iraq whom I had seen in the cancer wards and impoverished neighborhoods of Baghdad and Basra during a FOR interfaith peace mission there in 2000. The night after my release from the Tombs, I had a most vivid dream: I was visiting Sevagram, an ashram of Gandhi's in India. The Mahatma was showing me around the grounds and buildings. It was near sunset and the barren landscape was luminous in the golden glow of dusk. Gandhi seemed to be middle-aged, vigorous and joyful. He was smiling and wearing radiant white *khadi,* the homespun cloth that represented dignity and self-reliance. He moved his arm outward as he pointed out the different parts of the ashram. There the dream ended, but it remains strongly etched in my memory as a time when Gandhi was with me, as he is with all those who work nonviolently for a just and peaceful world.

We are indeed surrounded by a great cloud of witnesses of those who have gone before us and prepared the way

(Hebrews 12:1). It is my hope that this biography will help introduce the life and message of Gandhi to a new generation of persons searching for a genuine alternative to war, intolerance and injustice.

Richard Deats
Nyack, New York

Introduction

After studying in London to become a barrister, Mohandas Gandhi returned to Bombay, where he failed in his initial effort to practice law. His extreme shyness had made him a laughing stock in the courtroom. When he received a one-year contract with a Muslim firm in South Africa, however, he decided to go there to start over. In this new setting, he began to gain confidence. He had a keen mind and he showed an unusual ability to work fairly in the best interests of defendants and plaintiffs alike.

During his first year in South Africa, he traveled across the state of Natal on business for the firm. He began his ride alone in the first-class compartment, unaware that in apartheid South Africa first class accommodations were reserved for whites only. When the train had climbed high into the mountains and reached Martizburg, the capital of Natal, a European who entered the compartment saw the Indian seated there. He left to find a railroad official to remove him. A conductor informed Gandhi that he would have to move to the third-class car. Showing his first-class ticket

Gandhi protested, but the indifferent official demanded that he move. When Gandhi refused, a policeman was summoned to throw him and his luggage off the train. Gandhi sat up through the night shivering in the deserted train station, humiliated by the brutal treatment imposed upon him simply because of the color of his skin.

Rather than "knowing his place" the young Hindu lawyer determined never to allow such indignity to be visited upon himself or others again. Later he would reflect upon that evening in a lonely train station in the mountains of Natal as the most creative experience of his life, a turning point that indelibly shaped his future. Many people are broken and embittered by harsh, unjust treatment. Others such as Gandhi, like iron in a furnace, are purified and become steel.

Early Years

Gandhi's early life did not foreshadow his eventual role in reshaping India, and the world. He was born into a prosperous family on October 2, 1869, in Porbandar, a seaside town between Bombay and Karachi (the region of Gujarat, a state today tragically torn by Hindu-Muslim conflict). Mohandas was the youngest son of Karamchand and Putlibai Gandhi. His father, a politician, had no formal education but was incorruptible and loyal to his clan and family. Putlibai, his mother, was illiterate yet devout, even saintly; her sacrificial devotion to Hindu practices impressed her children deeply. Her religious fidelity influenced Mohandas throughout his life.

Extremely withdrawn, he did not do well in school. He was so shy that he would run home immediately after school to avoid his classmates. As he grew, he developed friendships but not all of them proved positive. When he was twelve he began smoking in secret and stole money from a servant and his brother to buy cigarettes. Ashamed of his conduct, he wrote a heart-felt confession to his father, who he feared would be furious. Instead, Karamchand wept. Mohandas later wrote that those tears washed his sin away and showed him the true meaning of *Ahimsa* ("non-hurting or non-violence"): "When such *Ahimsa* becomes all-embracing, it transforms everything it touches. There is no limit to its power" (Gandhi 1956, 28).

Child marriage was prevalent then and at thirteen, his parents arranged for him to marry Kasturbai Makanji, also thirteen. The child couple took their place in the large extended family. Mohandas sought to control his headstrong wife but she resisted his authority so they quarreled, sometimes going for days without speaking.

As a young husband Gandhi had many fears — the dark, ghosts, serpents. He was ashamed that an apparently fearless Kasturbai would go out at night. Rambha, a family servant, told the boy that it was best to deal with fear not by running from it but by standing one's ground, all the while repeating the mantram, *"Ram, Ram"* (God, God). Just as elephants going through a market will reach with their trunks for fruits and vegetables unless they are each given a stick of bamboo to hold, the mind is centered by a mantram that will carry it through fears, distractions and danger (Easwaran 1997, 117–19). Rambha's advice became the seed of a life-long practice that over time centered him in his devotion.

Although the skinny and unathletic Mohandas disliked sports, he had read that walking was good for one's health. As a result, he developed a habit that stayed with him throughout his life, giving him endurance and strength. His strongly vegetarian family did not countenance eating meat. He had a good friend, however, who was strong and excelled at sports. Popular belief held that eating meat made people strong (hence the meat-eating English could conquer that vastly larger nation of India) so Mohandas joined his friend in eating goat meat. It sickened him and led to terrible nightmares, but he continued for a year to eat meat secretly.

He rejected vegetarianism to build his physical strength, but he also ate meat as a way to reject the pomp and ceremony of religion. For a while he considered himself an atheist; nonetheless he listened carefully to his father's Parsi, Muslim, and Jain friends discussing their religious beliefs. Ritual and dogma turned him off but the morality of religion drew him in.

When it came time to prepare for a profession, Gandhi decided to follow a family tradition and study law, even though he doubted that he could succeed at it. A family friend told him of a three-year law course in England that not only was quick but brought with it the prestige and excitement of study abroad. The idea appealed to him, but presented obstacles. Some family members feared that Mohandas, immersed in Western dress, diet, and customs, would lose his Indian identity. He satisfied their anxieties by allowing a Jain monk to administer an oath that he would forswear women, wine, and meat while abroad.

In 1888 Kasturbai bore their first son, Harilal. A few months afterwards, Mohandas sailed for England; he was almost nineteen years old. For the trip he bought a Western style jacket and a tie and took along some fruit and sweets to supplement the ship's menu. The three-week sea journey to Southampton proved miserable. He could find little to eat on the meat-laden menu, and he had great trouble understanding English speakers. Isolated from the natural opportunities for conversation, his innate shyness only amplified his loneliness.

In London, Indian contacts helped him orient himself to the strange mores and routines of English life. He rigidly maintained his vegetarianism but found it difficult to

adjust to bland English food cooked without the spicy con-
diments used in India. He did seek, however, to adapt himself to other aspects of proper society. He purchased
English clothing, even a morning coat, silk shirts, a top hat,
spats, and a fancy cane. He took lessons in dancing, as well
as in French and elocution. He purchased a violin and
engaged a music teacher. After a few months, however, he
realized that he would only be in England a few years and
that he should focus himself not on the trappings of Western life, but on his legal studies. He decided to simplify his
life and trim his expenses, moving to smaller quarters and
preparing some of his own meals. To avoid paying carfare,
he began walking many miles every day, a practice that not
only saved money but kept him fit and healthy. His vow of
vegetarianism strengthened as he read widely on the subject. In time he stopped using the familiar spices and condi-
ments he had so enjoyed, saying that "the real seat of taste
was not in the tongue but in the mind" (Gandhi 1956, 56).

Throughout Gandhi's sojourn in England he never over-
came his shyness. In public meetings he would usually say
nothing at all. His reticence bothered him; on occasion he
wrote out remarks ahead of time but even then found it
impossible to read them. Although he could not conquer his
shyness, he came to see its positive side: "Experience has
taught me that silence is part of the spiritual discipline of
the votary of truth. Proneness to exaggerate, to suppress or
modify the truth, wittingly or unwittingly, is a natural
weakness of man, and silence is necessary in order to sur-
mount it" (Gandhi 1956, 62).

Inwardly he found a growing interest in religion, rejecting what he called "the Sahara of atheism." Given a Bible he
found that Genesis put him to sleep, and Numbers or Levit-
icus bored him. He loved the New Testament, however,
especially the Sermon on the Mount, which reminded him

of his beloved *Bhagavad Gita,* Hinduism's sacred book. When he read, "But I say unto you, that ye resist not evil; but whosoever shall smite thee on thy right cheek, turn to him the other also. And if any man take away thy coat let him have thy cloak too," the words went straight to his heart (Gandhi 1956, 68).

Gandhi found that legal studies came to him easily, but his conscientiousness caused him to prepare himself for the exams far beyond what was required. He passed the bar exams on June 10, 1891 and sailed for India on June 12. Upon returning, he found that his education provided scant practical help in practicing law, particularly because he knew so little of Indian history or of Hindu and Muslim law. Gandhi's lack of understanding of the Indian legal system coupled with his extreme shyness prevented him from representing his clients ably in court. At length he decided he needed a fresh start; when a firm of Porbandar Muslims, Dada Abdulla & Co., invited him to work in South Africa, he accepted readily. The only positive influence in his professional career in India had come not from his legal experience but from a wise businessman, Raychandbhai, who had devoted his life not to making money, but to seeking a way to meet God face to face.

Statue of Mahatma Gandhi at the King Center in Atlanta.
(photo by Richard Deats)

South Africa

In 1893, at the age of 23, Gandhi moved to Durban, a great South African coastal city with a significant Indian population. Indians, mostly low caste, had been emigrating to South Africa as indentured workers on the British-owned tea, coffee, and sugar plantations. After their five-year term of work ended many stayed on, but government regulations made their lives difficult. Gandhi did not find the work there challenging, but he relished the opportunity to see another part of the world.

Not long after arriving in Durban his firm sent him to handle a difficult case in Pretoria. On this train ride, while still new to South Africa, he encountered the brutal reality of racial prejudice. During that long, bitterly cold night in the Maritzburg station he came to a decision that set the course of his life: "The hardship to which I was subjected was superficial — only a symptom of the deep disease of colour prejudice. I should try, if possible, to root out the disease and suffer hardships in this process. Redress for wrongs I should seek only to the extent that would be necessary for

the removal of the colour prejudice" (Gandhi 1956, 112).
Gandhi had agreed to work in South Africa for only a year,
but this initial experience coupled with subsequent events
inspired and strengthened his resolve to fight the degrading
racism he discovered there. He stayed not one but
twenty-one years — from 1893 through 1914.

Gandhi remained in Pretoria for an entire year, one that
turned out to be momentous. Shortly after arriving, he called
a general meeting of Indians to discuss the prejudice they
were subjected to. He pledged to help them overcome it. Despite his shyness, his purpose and determination helped him
deliver a powerful speech. He admonished the audience to
improve themselves as much as possible by practicing truth-
fulness and fairness in their business dealings, transcending
caste and religious differences, learning English, and main-
taining cleanliness. He urged them to replace passivity with
self-esteem, industriousness and visible civic practices. This
would prepare them for the difficult struggle they faced: rich
or poor, educated or illiterate, laborers or professionals, Indians were all considered "coolies."

Indians were not allowed to vote; they had to carry a pass
after dark and could be pushed off a sidewalk to make way
for a white person; they had to remove their hats when talking to a white person; they had to pay an annual tax to stay
in the country; they were confined to segregated neighborhoods, where they generally could not own property. As
bad as the lot that Asians had to accept was, the native
black population endured even worse conditions. Gandhi
mused, "It has always been a mystery to me how men
can feel themselves honoured by the humiliation of their
fellow-beings" (Gandhi 1956, 155). His Indian audience
responded enthusiastically. Gandhi had a genius for defin-
ing both a situation and concrete ways of dealing with it. He
began to emerge as a leader in the Indian community.

He likewise matured as a lawyer while working on the case that brought him to Pretoria. It involved a dispute over accounting differences in extensive business transactions with a charge of fraudulent promissory notes. Both parties had hired the best attorneys and counsel. Gandhi studied all the fine points of the law, as well as learning bookkeeping. He saw the importance of getting reliable, trustworthy information. He learned that facts mean truth and that once we have the facts, the law comes to one's aid naturally. He also realized that an expensive case like this one could drag on indefinitely and exhaust the resources of both sides. He convinced the litigants to compromise and to turn their dispute over to an arbitrator. Dada Abdulla won the arbitration, but the opponent was allowed to pay off the sizable monetary award in installments.

Gandhi had finally achieved the confidence he needed not only to practice law but to help people come to fair and equitable solutions. These qualities strengthened his ability to help his people overcome the crippling racism that held them down. Although he had planned to return home to India, he saw he was needed for now in South Africa. A growing number of Indians were ready to follow his lead. He learned that the legislature of Natal, a British crown colony, was preparing a bill to prevent Indians from voting. He led an effort to petition the legislature to reject the bill, but it passed anyway. The bill could not take effect until approved by the British government, so Gandhi led a drive that gathered 10,000 signatures opposing the bill and sent it to London. The strong impact of the petition drive compelled the Colonial Office to veto the bill. Out of these efforts the Natal Indian Congress was organized in 1894, with Gandhi as its general secretary.

In 1896 Gandhi returned to India to arrange for moving his wife and three children to South Africa. In India he spoke publicly of the conditions in South Africa. In Natal, the press published exaggerated and sensationalized accounts of his speeches, so when Gandhi and his family landed in Durban, infuriated crowds of whites prevented them from disembarking — for nearly a month! Once ashore he narrowly escaped being lynched, such was the notoriety he had attained.

During the Boer War (1899–1902) Gandhi surprised many of his followers by organizing an ambulance corps to help the British. He said that the responsibilities of citizenship in the Commonwealth required that they show support with such an act of mercy. Gandhi chose to serve the British on the field of battle a second time during the 1906 Zulu rebellion. Leading the Indian stretcher-bearer corps, he was horrified at the inhuman, vicious treatment of the Zulus by the British. The experience led him to forswear cooperation with evil and to devote himself totally to serving humanity.

On a twenty-four hour train journey from Johannesburg to Durban, Gandhi read John Ruskin's *Unto This Last*. He credited reading Ruskin's book with "an instantaneous and practical transformation of my life" (Gandhi 1956, 299). Later, he translated it into his native Gujarati, entitling it *Sarvodaya* ("the welfare of all").

He summed up Ruskin's book as teaching three key maxims:

> — the good of the individual is contained in the good of all.
> — a lawyer's work has the same value as the barber's inasmuch as all have the same right of earning their livelihood from their work.
> — the life of labour, i.e., the life of the tiller of the soil and the handicraftsman, is the life worth living.
>
> (Gandhi 1956, 299)

While he said that he already knew the first and dimly perceived the second, the third was new to him. Their combination spoke powerfully to him and he put the book down "ready to reduce these principles to practice" — a decision typical of Gandhi's determination to live out what he had come to believe. He had no patience for words separated from deeds.

At the time Gandhi's weekly magazine, *Indian Opinion*, was experiencing financial difficulties. He decided to find a farm where the publication's workers could live, each receiving the same allowance "irrespective of colour or nationality" (Gandhi 1956, 300). His desire led him in 1904 to found the Phoenix Settlement, a farmhouse with some orange and mango trees on one hundred acres of land fourteen miles from Durban.

In this Spartan setting Gandhi put to work this "experiment with Truth," a little ashram of half a dozen families, European and Indian, who came from various religious backgrounds but shared a common ethical outlook. In this revolutionary community, everyone — men and women, caste and outcaste, European and Asian — possessed equal worth and had equal responsibilities. Departing from traditional patriarchy, women — "the suppressed half of humanity" — were not confined to domestic tasks; men also were expected to take on domestic work, and women were encouraged to participate in the full life and work of the community (Gandhi 1956, 301). The Phoenix Settlement foreshadowed the equal role women would play in the freedom movement both in South Africa and in India, where they took their places in the front ranks of the *satyagrahi*, receiving police blows, being arrested, and being sent to prison just like the men.

Gandhi developed vows for the community to pronounce at morning and evening prayers that "comprised nonviolence, truth, non-stealing, brahmacharya (chastity), non-possession, bread-labor, control of the palate, fearlessness, tolerance, equal respect for all religions, removal of untouchability and *swadesh* [i.e., being supportive of that which was indigenous] in the performance of ones duties."[1] Gandhi rejected the Indian practice of having outcastes do the sweeping, cleaning the latrines and other menial tasks. He thought everyone, including his wife Kasturbai, himself, and their children should share in these jobs. Kasturbai, particularly upset at having to empty the chamber pot of a former untouchable, fought with her husband over this. He was ready to expel her from the ashram when she brought him to his senses. His renunciation of the ideology of patriarchy would require years of experiment and struggle to be accepted in practice. He realized that he had to control his demanding and even violent temperament. In fact, he came to desire that he relinquish all his desires and urges — dietary, sexual, emotional — to a higher purpose. This he found in the practice of *Brahmacharya*, literally the search after God, or *Brahma,* signifying "control of all the senses and at all places in thought, word and deed" (Gandhi 1956, 208–11). At the age of 37, he told Kasturbai of his desire to be celibate and she consented willingly. Celibacy involved far more than giving up sex, however. He pledged himself to simplicity and poverty, living like the poorest Indian. He no longer needed the English clothes he had thought necessary for practicing law; a simple *dhoti* (loincloth) was quite sufficient and it demonstrated identification with the poor. He read voraciously about dietary matters and experimented with the simplest healthy diet he could take. He was not

---

1. *The Collected Works of Mahatma Gandhi*, 1:vii. (Hereafter, this set of books will be referred to as *CWMG*, followed by the volume number and page reference).

just vegetarian; he ate only to sustain his bodily needs, not to please his taste buds. Moreover, he would fast for purification and penance. His renunciation became increasingly complete. He observed, "Only give up a thing when you want some other condition so much that the thing has no longer any attraction for you" (Gandhi 1956, 317). His passion to see God face to face led him to bring his desires under control.

In 1906 he led the first *satyagraha* campaign. In the state of Transvaal, the white government had announced as part of the effort to undermine the basic civil rights of the Asian community an onerous Asiatic Registration Ordinance that would require every Indian immigrant to be fingerprinted and registered. Thousands of Indians joined Gandhi in Johannesburg to protest the Ordinance. They came to the meeting ready for violence but Gandhi moved them to respond enthusiastically to his call for nonviolent resistance, using the newly coined word *satyagraha*. He urged them to resist, without violence, even if their death was the result.

Gandhi saw that *satyagraha* was "the moral equivalent of war," to use the term coined by William James. As the campaign spread throughout South Africa, Indians displayed a willingness to counter violence with nonviolence, hatred with love, and contempt with courage. They accepted arrest in a civil fashion, showing a respect for truth and honoring the purpose of good laws, but rejecting bad laws as violent and unjust.

As the campaign grew, Gandhi met with the head of the Transvaal government, the renowned Boer War general Jan Christiaan Smuts. Without hostility Gandhi told Smuts plainly that the truth was on their side. Resistance would continue and their indefatigable will and their nonviolence would prevail. Over time, Smuts's attitude changed from contempt to grudging admiration. Even in the face of strong opposition, Gandhi treated Smuts with respect. When Smuts imprisoned Gandhi, the Indian leader made him a pair of sandals!

Gandhi's first imprisonment came in 1908 when he was sentenced to two months in a Johannesburg jail. In the library there he read Henry David Thoreau's essay, "Civil Disobedience." It impressed him deeply. Thoreau had gone to jail for refusing to pay taxes that would help fund US aggression against Mexico. It was not enough to *say* you oppose evil, wrote Thoreau: you must take action.

Gandhi was released when Smuts pledged that the Ordinance would be repealed. But when Smuts broke his promise, Gandhi proceeded to organize his second *satyagraha* campaign that called for Indians to burn their certificates of registration. Smuts sent Gandhi to prison a second, then a third time. During this period a second ashram was established, this one near Johannesburg. Tolstoy Farm served the needs of the families of prisoners by providing a safe space for community, gardening and other self-help projects. Gandhi named it after the great Russian pacifist with whom he had been carrying on a lengthy correspondence. Leo Tolstoy's *The Kingdom of God is Within You* also profoundly influenced Gandhi's outlook.

Increasingly, Gandhi came to understand the importance of *swadeshi* (i.e., people using that which was indigenous to them). He maintained that economic self-help, including the refusal to be dependent upon the oppressors' products, was crucial for the Indians in South Africa to regain their self-sufficiency and their self-respect. At Tolstoy Farm Gandhi began fasting, not just for reasons of health but as a means of self-restraint. His close friend and colleague, Hermann Kallenbach — a Jew — joined in fasting, just as he had entered into Gandhi's other experiments with Truth. Muslims, Christians, and Parsis fasted as well. While Gandhi maintained a water-only fast, the Muslims followed their custom of fasting from sunup to sundown. In addition to giving example by fasting, Gandhi provided literary and vocational training for all. As at Phoenix Settlement, there were no servants, no outcastes to do menial tasks. All joined in the work. Kallenbach, a skilled horticulturist, helped to establish a model garden. Training of the spirit through hymns and moral lessons was also a part of their daily life. All the teachers were expected to set a particular example so as to set the children on a godly path. Gandhi — or "Bapu" (Father) as he was called — set aside each Monday for his personal day of silence, a weekly withdrawal in order to keep his life centered on God.

In 1912 Indian women entered into a campaign to fight legislation that would in effect invalidate Indian marriages. The women urged miners in the Transvaal to strike. Strike they did, and many of the protesting miners went to jail along with the women and Gandhi. This third *satyagraha* campaign succeeded in winning over increasing numbers of the European community, both in South Africa as well as abroad.

Etching done during the cold war by E. Tacke, quaker artist in East Berlin

Gandhi's Religion

Gandhi's goal in life was to see God face to face. By the
time he returned to India from South Africa he had formed
his basic religious outlook, but until the end of his life he
kept experimenting with Truth, always growing, always
searching, always testing; hence the subtitle of his autobiography: *The Story of My Experiments With Truth*. These experiments led him to certain basic convictions:

> To me God is Truth and Love; God is ethics and
> morality; God is fearlessness. God is the source of
> Light and Life and yet God is above and beyond
> all these. God is conscience. God is even the athe-
> ism of the atheist. For in God's boundless love
> God permits the atheist to live. God is the
> searcher of hearts. God transcends speech and
> reason. God knows us and our hearts better than
> we do ourselves. God does not take us at our word
> for God knows that we often do not mean it, some
> knowingly and others unknowingly. God is a per-
> sonal God to those who need God's personal pres-

ence. God is embodied in those who need God's
touch. God is the purest essence. God simply *is* to
those who have faith. God is all things to all people. (*Young India,* March 5, 1925 in Mohandas K.
Gandhi, *My Religion.* Ahmedabad: Navajivan
Publishing House, 1971, 38)

Three years later, he wrote:

> I do simply perceive that whilst everything
> around me is ever changing, ever dying, there is
> underlying all that change a living power that is
> changeless, that holds all together, that creates,
> dissolves, and recreates. That informing power or
> spirit is God. And since nothing else I see merely
> through the sense can or will persist, God alone is.
> And is this power benevolent or malevolent? I
> see it as purely benevolent. For I can see that in
> the midst of death life persists, in the midst of
> untruth truth persists, in the midst of darkness
> life persists. Hence I gather that God is Life,
> Truth, Light. God is Love. God is the Supreme
> Good. (*Young India,* October 11, 1928; in Gandhi
> 1955, 37)
> I have found that life persists in the midst of
> destruction and therefore there must be a higher
> law than that of destruction. Only under that law
> would a well-ordered society be intelligible and
> life worth living. And if that is the law of life, we
> have to work it out in daily life. Whenever there
> are jars, whenever you are confronted with an
> opponent, conquer him with love — in this crude
> manner I have worked it out in my life. That does
> not mean that all my difficulties are solved. Only
> I have found that this law of love has answered as

the law of destruction has never done. The more I work at this law, the more I feel delight in life, delight in the scheme of this universe. It gives me a peace and a meaning of the mysteries of nature that I have no power to describe. (*Young India,* October 1, 1931; in Gandhi 1955, 62)

Religious belief did not lead Gandhi to seek otherworldly escape, but caused him to root himself always more steadfastly in the needs of the world: "I could not be leading a religious life unless I identified myself with the whole of humanity, and that I could not do unless I took part in politics. The whole gamut of humanity's activities constitutes an indivisible whole. You cannot divide social, economic, political, and purely religious work into watertight compartments. I do not know any religion apart from human activity. It provides a moral basis to all other activities which they would otherwise lack, reducing life to a maze of 'sound and fury signifying nothing' " (*Harijan,* December 24, 1938; in Gandhi 1955, 343).

In particular, serving humanity meant serving the poor: "My experience tells me that the Kingdom of God is within us, and that we can realize it not by saying, 'Lord, Lord,' but by doing God's will and work. If therefore we wait for the Kingdom to come as something coming from outside, we shall be sadly mistaken. Do you know that there are thousands of villages where people are starving and which are on the brink of ruin? If we would listen to the voice of God, I assure you we would hear God say that we are taking God's name in vain if we do not think of the poor and help them. If you cannot render the help that they need, it is no use talking of service of God and service of the poor. Try to identify yourselves with the poor by actually helping them" (*Young India,* March 10, 1927; in *CWMG* 33:193).

Gandhi was convinced that we practice our religion and that we help the poor through the same approach — nonviolence. In 1935 he wrote to the Fellowship of Reconciliation:

> Nonviolence is the greatest force humanity has been endowed with. Truth is the only goal humanity has. For God is none other that Truth. But Truth cannot be and never will be reached except through nonviolence.
>
> That which distinguishes humanity from all other animals is our capacity to be nonviolent. And humanity fulfills this mission only to the extent that humanity is nonviolent and no more. Humanity has no doubt many other gifts. But if they do not subserve the main purpose — the development of the spirit of nonviolence in humanity — they but drag humanity down lower than the brute, a status from which humanity has only just emerged.
>
> The cry for peace will be a cry in the wilderness, so long as the spirit of nonviolence does not dominate millions of men and women.
>
> An armed conflict between nations horrifies us. But the economic war is no better than an armed conflict. This is like a surgical operation. An economic war is prolonged torture. And its ravages are no less terrible than those depicted in the literature on war properly so-called. We think nothing of the other because we are used to its deadly effects. . . .
>
> The movement against war is sound. I pray for its success. But I cannot help the gnawing fear that the movement will fail, if it does not touch the root of all evil — man's greed. (M. K. Gandhi,

"Non-violence — The Greatest Force," in *The World Tomorrow,* October 5, 1926, 143)

The nonviolent life "is possible of fulfillment only by a strong, and if need be, a long course of self-purification and suffering" (Gandhi 1970, 58). Noncooperation with evil, civil disobedience that breaks unjust laws, standing for unpopular truth, laying down one's life for the oppressed and forgotten: these lead to suffering that is the soil in which the seeds of love, truth and peace spring to life.

The votary of nonviolence practices *Ahimsa* (harmlessness), the way of love. A life based on *Ahimsa* is consistent: means and ends are inter-related. "The means may be likened to a seed, the end to a tree; there is the same inviolable connection between the means and the end as there is between the seed and the tree" (Gandhi1960, 75). Many affirm noble goals but then justify violent actions to defend and advance those goals. An expedient approach like this is antithetical to Gandhi's, which holds that the end is actually pre-existent in the means. Ignoble means subvert the noble end. Good overcomes evil, just as water puts out fire.

Having grown up in a Hindu home with an especially devout mother, Gandhi loved Hinduism's sacred book, *The Bhagavad Gita.* Throughout his life he identified himself as a Hindu, but he remained remarkably open to Truth wherever he found it. He believed all religions led to Truth. "I believe in the fundamental truth of all the great religions of the world. I believe they are all God-given, and I believe that they were necessary for the people to whom these religions were revealed. And I believe that, if only we could all of us read the scriptures of different faiths from the standpoint of the followers of those faiths, we should find that they were at bottom all one and were all helpful to one another" (*Harijan,* February 16, 1934; in Gandhi 1960, 55).

Gandhi honored all religions and spent his life working for religious understanding and collaboration. He maintained a life-long affection for Muslims, who were a large presence in India. Hindu-Muslim relations concerned him right up to his last days. Abdul Ghaffar Khan, "the Frontier Gandhi," a close disciple of Gandhi, was very effective in interpreting nonviolence from the Muslim faith. Although he thought that "the followers of Islam are too free with the sword," Gandhi understood that Islam is essentially a religion of peace. The violence sometimes associated with Islam "is not due to the teaching of the Koran. This is due, in my opinion, to the environment in which Islam was born" (*Young India,* January 20, 1927; in Gandhi 1955, 27).

During his legal studies in London, Gandhi had met many Christians. He read the Bible and visited their churches. The message of Jesus went right to his heart, so much so that he placed the Sermon on the Mount alongside *The Bhagavad Gita* in importance. "Jesus expressed," said Gandhi, "as no other could, the spirit and will of God. It is in this sense that I see Him and recognize Him as the Son of God. And because the life of Jesus has the significance and the transcendency to which I have alluded, I believe that He belongs not solely to Christianity, but to the entire world, to all races and people — it matters little under what flag, name or doctrine they may work, profess a faith, or worship a God inherited from their ancestors" (Gandhi 1955, 25).

While in South Africa, Gandhiji (a diminutive form of affection often used by followers of Gandhi's teachings) decided to reject the efforts of Christians to convert him when he had gone to hear Charles F. Andrews preach and was not allowed in the church because of the color of his skin! This experience and others like it convinced him that the way he saw Christians living did not correspond to the way of Jesus. He wrote,

I consider Western Christianity in its practical
working a negation of Christ's Christianity. I cannot conceive Jesus, if he was living in the flesh in
our midst, approving of modern Christian organizations, public worship, or modern ministry. If
Christians will simply cling to the Sermon on the
Mount, which was delivered not merely to the
peaceful disciples but a groaning world, they
would not go wrong, and they would find that no
religion is false, and that if they act according to
their lights and in the fear of God, they would not
need to worry about organizations, forms of worship, and ministry. . . . Cooperation with the
forces of Good and noncooperation with the
forces of evil are the two things we need for a good
and pure life, whether it is called Hindu, Muslim
or Christian. (*Young India*, September 22, 1921;
in Gandhi 1986, 21)

E. Stanley Jones, a well-known Methodist missionary
who deeply loved India and worked there for many years,
once asked Gandhi, "How can we make Christianity natu-
ralized in India, not a foreign thing, identified with a foreign government and a foreign people, but a part of the
national life of India and contributing its power to India's
uplift?" Gandhi responded: "First, I would suggest that all
of you Christians, missionaries and all, must begin to live
more like Jesus Christ. Second, practice your religion without adulterating it or toning it down. Third, emphasize love
and make it your working force, for love is central in Christianity. Fourth, study the non-Christian religions more
sympathetically to find the good that is within them, in
order to have a more sympathetic approach to the people."
These words deeply influenced Jones, particularly Gandhi's
insistence on love not as a mere sentiment but as a working

force. According to Jones, Gandhi understood that Christians should "make the Cross operative in the political and economic as well as in the religious (spheres of life). This," said Jones, "is the deepest challenge that has ever come to the Christian world, for it means nothing less than abandoning the whole war system and adopting *Satyagraha* instead" (Jones 1948, 51–53).

Finally, Gandhi believed that prayer and fasting should undergird every aspect of daily life. The practice of nonviolence requires it. "If you would ask God to help you, you would go to God in all your nakedness, approach God without reservations, also without fear or doubts as to how God can help a fallen being like you. God, who has helped millions who have approached him, is God going to desert you? God makes no exceptions whatsoever, and you will find that every one of your prayers will be answered. I am telling this out of my personal experience. I have gone through the purgatory. Seek first the Kingdom of Heaven, and everything will be added to you" (*Young India*, April 4, 1929; in Gandhi 1955, 93).

Gandhi practiced fasting — "the sincerest form of prayer" — as the companion to his other religious practices. He fasted in order to identify with the poor and hungry, to heighten his sense of contrition for his own failures as well as the failures of others, and to arouse their awareness of the nonviolence that God claimed from them and their actions.

At times, Gandhi pledged a fast unto death, relenting only when the situation changed significantly. He used fasting as the principal method for expressing his belief in the redemptive suffering of the innocent. As he reminded Christians and all people of faith, "God did not bear the cross only 1900 years ago but he bears it today and he dies and is resurrected from day to day" (*Young India*, August 11, 1927; in Gandhi 1960, 55). He also expressed this belief in his identification with Christ's crucifixion and in his great love for the hymn, "When I Survey the Wondrous Cross." Gandhiji summed up the religious aim of his life this way: "The opinions I have formed and the conclusions I have arrived at are not final. I may change them tomorrow; I have nothing new to teach the world. Truth and nonviolence are as old as the hills. All I have done is to try experiments in both on as vast a scale as I could do. In doing so I have sometimes erred and learnt by my errors. Life and its problems have thus become to me so many experiments in the practice of truth and nonviolence" (*Harijan,* March 28, 1936; in Gandhi 1955, 164).

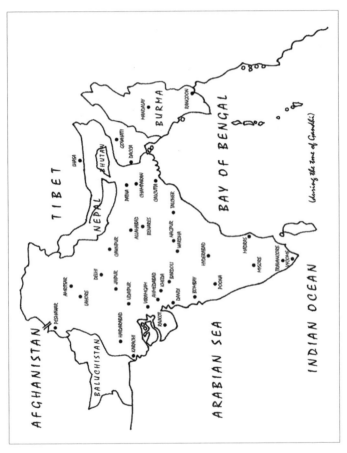

India during the Gandhi era

Return to India

In 1914, at 44 years of age, Gandhi returned to India. The fame that preceded him produced a tumultuous welcome. Nevertheless, he needed time to get reacquainted with his motherland. He had been away for twenty-one years, immersed in the struggles of South Africa's Indians.

He decided to take a full year to travel over the subcontinent and to reflect. With his family and some members of the Phoenix Settlement, he planned to live in an ashram. Until they could find a permanent site they could call their own, they stayed at Shantiniketan close to the great Bengali poet, Rabindranath Tagore. Over time, he and Gandhi became close friends. He would come to love and live by this sentence from Tagore's hymn: "If they answer not thy call, walk alone, walk alone." At length Gandhi decided to establish his own ashram in Gujurat, near Ahmedabad. He felt he could work most effectively speaking his native tongue. In addition Ahmedabad was the ancient center of handloom spinning and Gandhi felt it would be receptive to the revival of hand-spinning that he favored. They named it "the Satyagraha Ashram": "Our creed was devotion to truth, and our business was the search for and insistence on truth. I wanted to acquaint India with the method I had tried in South Africa, and I desired to test in India the extent to which its application might be possible" (Gandhi 1956, 396). The initial twenty-five members of the ashram were soon joined by an untouchable family. The prejudice in the outside community, in which caste was such a determining factor in all aspects of life, caused hostility and a precipitous decline in monetary support. An unexpected donation, a handsome sum from a wealthy Orthodox Hindu, averted the crisis. His support suggested the erosion of the stigma of untouchability at least among a few of the Orthodox. The presence of the untouchable family proved a severe test for some members of the ashram who had difficulty adjusting to such a radical break with tradition. The crisis helped the community grow, however; it tested the strength of their beliefs and they prevailed.

Gandhi's life and teachings illustrate his practical idealism. Ideals were not abstractions: they were to be lived, experimented with. At the ashrams members entered into a community where men and women, persons of different castes and origins and stations in life, vowed to live and work together. As problems arose — such as untouchables coming to live there — Gandhi believed the members had to work them out patiently but surely, dealing both with the way they related to the untouchables and their inner violence that led them to consider the untouchables, if not less than human, then beneath the others in the community.

In 1917 tension arose when the owners of the textile mills in Ahmedabad decided against giving the workers a previously agreed-upon fifty per cent cost of living increase. Some of the mill owners asked Gandhi to help resolve the problem. Gandhi called for arbitration. The owners decided to accept an increase of twenty per cent but the workers demanded the full fifty per cent. Gandhi, who knew both the mill owners and the workers, carefully studied the situation and said that thirty five per cent would be a fair compromise.

When the arbitration broke down, Gandhi called for a nonviolent campaign of *satyagraha*. Despite their strike, he called for the employees to engage in constructive work so they would not have to ask for charity, harming their self-respect.

After a twenty-one-day strike, the mill owners accepted binding arbitration. Gandhi ended his fast with the settlement that led to the establishment of a strong trade union that included social services for its members. The mill owners and the workers mutually arrived at a thirty-five per cent wage increase. A wealthy woman from one of the mill owners' homes, Anasya Sarabhai, added an important dimension to the campaign as she organized a labor union that formed a number of schools, some of which were for Untouchables (Gandhi 1956, 430–32).

SIN OF SECRECY

YOUNG INDIA

Published Every Wednesday.

(Edited by M. K. Gandhi)

| New Series Vol. II, No. 51. | AHMEDABAD, WEDNESDAY, DECEMBER 22nd 1920. | Price Two Annas Per Copy. |

CO-OPERATION THROUGH COERCION?

(By L. A. Jidwani.)

The newspaper *Young India* was founded by Gandhi in 1919

Turning Point in the Struggle

Gandhi's support for the British during World War I changed dramatically in 1919 when the Raj enacted the infamous Rowlatt Bills. This colonial legislation mandated detention without trial for anyone suspected of sedition, and dealt harshly with anyone possessing seditious materials. The British were determined to silence anyone who questioned their wartime policies, but the extremity and undemocratic nature of these bills set off a storm in India. They made a farce of the rule of law and other democratic claims by the empire.

Gandhi responded swiftly and strongly, mounting nationwide opposition to this repressive legislation. He called for a *hartal,* or work stoppage, to demonstrate Indian determination to resist. Gandhi proclaimed April 6 as a national day of fasting, including rallies and a general strike. The response was electric: prayer and fasting, processions and meetings, the closing of shops and businesses spread across India.

The strike thrust Gandhi onto the national stage as the unmistakable leader of India's liberation struggle. From the ashram in Ahmedabad, the *hartal* fanned out to Calcutta, Madras and Bombay. Gandhi traveled the country, raising consciousness and building the *satyagraha* campaign.

Supporters of the *hartal* took a pledge that said, "We shall refuse civilly to obey these laws" by "faithfully follow(ing) truth and refrain(ing) from violence to life, person or property" (Mary King 1999, 43). This pledge was not to be taken lightly: no one was to commit civil disobedience without first fasting for twenty-four hours. Forbidden books, such as *Sarvodaya* (Gandhi's Gujarati version of Ruskin's *Unto This Last*) and Gandhi's booklet *Hind Swaraj (Free India)*, gained wide distribution. Gandhi felt that printing and selling them openly was an easy but forceful way of committing civil disobedience and educating increasing numbers of people in the process, as well as making money to be used in the freedom struggle (Gandhi 1956, 455–62).

Forceful resistance by the police to the campaign triggered counter-violence by the protesters, who burned buildings and killed some police and soldiers. Gandhi condemned the violence as wrong and counter-productive, but his words could not contain the angry mood. The British imposed martial law in Ahmedabad as well as in Amritsar and Lahore. In Amritsar, on April 13, Brigadier General Reginald Dyer ordered his troops to open fire on thousands of unarmed men, women and children who had gathered in a walled area to celebrate a religious festival. When the machine guns stopped, 379 persons lay dead and many more were wounded.

Government callousness, including Dyer's lack of remorse, only deepened the anti-British fury. As if the massacre were not infuriating enough, after the assault on an Englishwoman in Armritsar, British authorities issued a "crawling order" that commanded all Indians who passed the site of the attack to get down on all fours and crawl "like worms" past the spot. Gandhi labeled the British actions "lawless repression" (Gandhi 1956, 471). The cruel oppression by the Raj in India, now made public, unleashed an irreversible tide for freedom

At the same time, however, Gandhi expressed his horror at the *Indian* violence that contradicted the call to *satyagraha*. He undertook a penitential three-day fast, taking the suffering onto himself. He had over-estimated the people's readiness and commitment to adhere to *means* that were compatible with the *end* being sought. A goal such as freedom, no matter how noble, cannot be achieved through unworthy means.

Gandhi did not try to defend himself from criticism concerning the violence and mayhem that had followed his call to *satyagraha*. Always his sternest critic, he quickly acknowledged his own failures and bad decisions. He labelled his actions a "Himalayan miscalculation": the people did not fully understand nor were they committed to *satyagraha*. He had no pre-determined, foolproof road to freedom. The way would be nonviolent, but it was always an *experiment with truth,* to be tested and refined again and again. When he admitted publicly his missteps he was subjected to ridicule. He maintained, however, "I have always held that it is only when one sees one's own mistakes with a convex lens, and does just the reverse in the case of others, that one is able to arrive at a just relative estimate of the two. I further believe that a scrupulous and conscientious observance of this rule is necessary for one who wants to be a *Satyagrahi*" (Gandhi 1956, 469).

Gandhi felt that he had to work far harder to broaden the understanding of the oppression by the British, to deepen the understanding of *satyagraha,* and to help the people recover their dignity and self-reliance that imperial policies

had so undermined. Indefatigably, he traveled the length
and breadth of India, writing all the time. In 1919 he
became editor of the English-language newspaper *Young
India* and of the Gujarati newspaper *Navajivan.* Along with
his many other writings, these newspapers became vehicles
for a steady outpouring of Gandhi's thought. His constant
writing and correspondence provides a rich legacy of his
thinking right up to the time of his death.

Many different causes concerned him. He worked for
Hindu-Muslim unity. He condemned what he called "the
curse of untouchability" and the rigid caste practices that
separated people. He called for noncooperation with British institutions across the board: self-reliance required Indians to no longer depend upon nor even cooperate with the
British Raj. Getting Indians to stop wearing British-made
goods required the rebuilding of village cottage industry to
produce *khadi,* or home-spun cloth. Farmers worked the
land only part of the year; the revival of spinning could put
their energies to use during the dry season. This would stim-
ulate life in India's 700,000 villages and bring employment
to poor people, especially women. But all persons working
for the freedom of India, including Gandhi and the members of the ashrams were to take up spinning, because it provided rigorous discipline, revived a useful skill, provided an
alternative to imported cloth, and unified the people across
class and caste, gender and status.

As Gandhi wrote and worked and organized, he drew
from the deep well of spirituality that motivated him and
shared what he found there with his readers and the wider
public:

> To see the universal and all-pervading Spirit of
> Truth face to face one must be able to love the
> meanest of creatures as oneself. And a person who

aspires after that cannot afford to keep out of any field of life. That is why my devotion to Truth has drawn me into the field of politics; and I can say without the slightest hesitation, and yet in all humility, that those who say that religion has nothing to do with politics do not know what religion means.

Identification with everything that lives is impossible without self-purification. Without self-purification the observance of the law of Ahimsa must remain an empty dream: God can never be realized by one who is not pure of heart. Self-purification therefore must mean purification in all the walks of life. And being highly infectious, purification of oneself necessarily leads to the purification of one's surroundings (Gandhi 1956, 504).

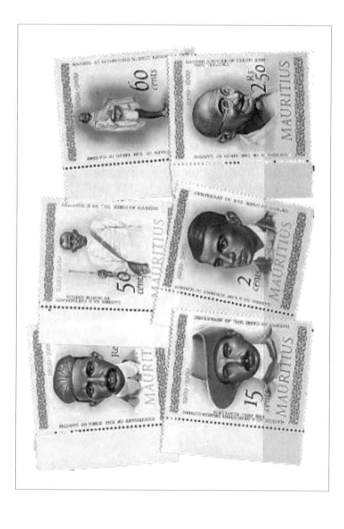

The Freedom
Movement Spreads

The freedom movement permeated India like leaven in dough. The public actions that Gandhi encouraged kept the British in a defensive posture. They found resistance growing everywhere. Gandhi's writings and speeches, along with his actions, convinced the British that he had to be stopped. On March 10, 1922 he was arrested for sedition and after a perfunctory trial was sentenced to six years in prison. At the trial in Ahmedebad, the eloquent courtroom statement of this once shy lawyer moved even the British judge to remark on Gandhi's persuasive sincerity.

Gandhi entered prison gladly. He wrote of "the cheerful acceptance of jail discipline and its attendant hardships," saying that jail becomes a temple when God is honored and worshiped (Gandhi 1970, 47–48). Those who practiced civil disobedience did not try to evade the law nor to escape prison. The campaign of *satyagraha* required that citizens follow the law, but to resist it if it became oppressive. If resistance included imprisonment, so be it. Prison became transformed into a place where one suffered for a just cause. Enforced confinement did not imprison the human spirit, but provided the opportunity for deepened commitment and discipline. During his six-year sentence, Gandhi wrote the first part of his autobiography as well as *Satyagraha in South Africa.*

Gandhi suffered acute appendicitis. Although he felt that he should serve his entire term, he was released after serving two years of his six-year sentence to have an appendectomy. The *satyagraha* movement was spreading but faced tenacious obstacles. Despite Gandhi's efforts for Hindu-Muslim unity, deep religious and cultural differences between the two communities undermined the road to freedom. The Hindus had taken up speaking the English language of the Empire, unlike the Muslims. Over time this gave the Hindus economic and political advantages. Hindus venerated the cow as sacred, but Muslims approved of the slaughter of cows for food. Such differences turned each community away from a common goal of independence from the British.

A bloody outbreak of violence between Hindus and Muslims in the fall of 1924 — the year Gandhi was released from prison — led him to undertake a twenty-one-day fast. The strong, positive response to the fast resulted in a unity conference in Delhi that condemned the violence and passed forceful resolutions for unity and freedom. In turn, Gandhi ended his fast.

The Vykom *Satyagraha*

Gandhi's opposition to British imperial policies did not prevent him from also dealing with internal Indian traditions and practices that kept the people in bondage. One of the worst of these traditions was untouchability.

This ancient curse of Indian society and wicked perversion of Hinduism placed millions of Indians even below the lowest castes; they were *out*castes — totally outside the caste system, kept that way from birth to death. Untouchables were restricted to the most menial jobs, such as sweeping streets, removing cow dung, and cleaning latrines. They were segregated into the poorest areas of communities and were considered so despicable that even their shadows were a defilement. Tradition forbade even *touching* such a person! Gandhi referred to the untouchables as *harijans,* children of God.

In 1924 Gandhi received a call for help from Travancore in the far south in India (in the state now known as Kerala). A Hindu temple was located in the village of Vykom where *brahmins* (the priestly caste) worshiped. There was an outcaste area not far away, but the untouchables who lived there were forbidden to use the road that passed by the temple, even though that was the way to their homes.

Reformers in the area who wanted to change this evil practice asked Gandhi for help. Although Gandhi's illness prevented him from coming, he provided guidance for what became known as the Vykom *satyagraha*. Supporters of the outcastes announced that public roads should be for all the public. With their allies in front, untouchables walked down the road directly in front of the temple, triggering a violent response from *brahmins* who attacked them and called in the police.

To sustain the campaign an ashram was set up nearby to provide a place where participants in the *satyagraha* could pray, receive training, and study. As Gandhi always wanted the freedom movement to include constructive programs, the ashram also taught spinning. By increasing their self-reliance, participants also began to restore their dignity.

A police cordon established to "protect" the temple was met by rotating shifts of volunteers who held vigil in front of the police and pleaded their case with them. The protest continued day and night for months, even when monsoon rains so flooded the road that the police took to boats while those holding vigil stood their ground, even when water reached up to their shoulders.

For sixteen months the campaign continued with the help of thousands of volunteers. In the pages of *Young India* Gandhi wrote about the campaign, further spreading understanding of *satyagraha* throughout India.

The end of the campaign itself vividly illustrates Gandhi's approach. He did not want to defeat his enemies but to *win them over* in the process, helping them see the inherent justice in what the oppressed were seeking. When the police barricades finally came down, the untouchables waited until the *brahmins* themselves accepted the dramatic change, as they did with these words: "We cannot resist any longer the prayers that have been made to us, and we are ready to receive the untouchables" (Shridharani 1939, 92). Shridharani's *War Without Violence* (89–92) contains an important account of this campaign. Decades later, civil rights activists in the United States trying to end legal segregation used Shridharani's book as a training manual. Campaigns such as the Montgomery Bus Boycott showed how the freedom movement in India inspired and instructed succeeding generations to win their freedom through nonviolence.

The Spinning Wheel

The spinning wheel in the center of India's flag is a constant reminder of the part it played in the nation's liberation. The heart-breaking poverty of India's masses convinced Gandhi that a return to the spinning wheel would provide a godly path to self-reliance, economic stability, and social harmony. The spinning wheel represented both political and spiritual realities. "Spinning and weaving cloth" would, he said, "clothe mother India."

Spinning provided an antidote to the widespread attitude that those with means and education should not stoop to performing manual labor — an attitude that many still hold. Gandhi advocated villagers taking up spinning, but he also maintained that people from every station in life should engage daily in at least thirty minutes of spinning, binding together all members of society into the renewal of Indian life and well-being.

The universality of taking up spinning developed unity between religions; it brought women out of seclusion, giving them renewed dignity; it even enhanced the worship, for God is met in the eyes of the poor.

Furthermore, spinning had a renewing, ripple effect on village life: "It is not merely the wages earned by the spinners that are to be counted but it is the whole reconstruction that follows in the wake of the spinning wheel. The village weaver, the village dyer, the village washerman, the village blacksmith, the village carpenter, all and many others will then find themselves reinstated in their ancient dignity, as is already happening wherever the spinning wheel has gained a footing" (*Young India*, March 10, 1927; in Fischer 1962, 225).

All were to wear *khadi* or homespun — not just the poor but certainly those working for independence, including members of the Congress Party. In fact, Gandhi would accept the presidency of the Congress Party only if the members agreed to wear *khadi,* saying, "It is impossible for us to establish a living vital connection with the masses unless we will work for them, through them and in their midst, not as their patrons but as their servants (*Young India,* February 3, 1927; in Fischer 1962, 22). Increasingly, this meant refusing to wear imported British cloth, even though it was attractive and relatively inexpensive. Imported cloth sucked the lifeblood out of India; self-reliance would replace the need for it.

In January 1929 Gandhi called for the public not only to boycott foreign cloth but to burn it as well. He said just as an infected house in Johannesburg had been burned down during an outbreak of the plague, so it was necessary for public and private burnings of the foreign cloth that had devastated the economy of India. On March 4, Gandhi staged a dramatic event in Calcutta to focus public attention on the importance of wearing *khadi*. He urged people to throw their foreign-made clothing onto a bonfire. Although the demonstration was peaceful and orderly, the police rushed in and beat the people with *lathi* (long wooden poles, often tipped with metal). Even though he had clearly said that burning cloth was not civil disobedience as it was not illegal, Gandhi was arrested.

Gandhi's arrests drew great attention, but they should not obscure the constructive program that lay at the heart of his work. Nonviolence is not so much about resisting evil, but about the daily concrete efforts to build a renewed, healthy, self-sustaining society. The patient, quiet, laborious efforts of thousands upon thousands of people awakening to their indispensable place in a truly free India wove a new tapestry of life that gave them hope and renewed vision.

The Salt March

The tide for *swaraj* — independence — proved unstoppable. The Congress Party proclaimed January 26, 1930 as Independence Day, designating Gandhi to plan and lead civil disobedience campaigns to hasten real independence. At the top of his agenda were the nefarious Salt Laws. The British Raj, in its attempt to control the entire subcontinent, had declared a monopoly on the production and sale of salt. As everyone used salt in their diet, even the poorest of the poor, the tax enriched the empire but further impoverished the people. They were not even allowed to make salt for themselves from seawater.

Mobilizing, educating, and training the people for a strategic *satyagraha* campaign, Gandhi called for every province to take part in a frontal assault on the Salt Laws. Marveling at Gandhi's call, Nehru said, "Salt suddenly became a mystical word" (Nehru 1941, 157).

Gandhi believed that attempting to negotiate with the responsible authorities prior to civil disobedience was essential, and so informed Lord Irwin, the Viceroy of India, of the plan and the reason for it. Receiving only a formal reply from Irwin's secretary, Gandhi challenged the monopoly and tax on salt in the most dramatic way possible: he called for a march from Ahmedebad to the seacoast at Dandi — 241 miles! Gandhi, now 61, and seventy-eight other *satyagrahis* set out on March 12, 1930. "We act on behalf of the hungry, the naked, the unemployed. We are marching in the name of God," said Gandhi (Fischer 1950, 267). The diverse group, which included untouchables, was deeply experienced in nonviolence. Along the way, Gandhi spoke in each village about the struggle for freedom and their part in it. He found time at the end of each day to write in his diary as well as to sit at his spinning wheel and spin.

As *khadi*-clad *satyagrahis* peacefully marched, hundreds, then thousands joined the original seventy-nine. They touched the hearts and minds of the villagers along the route as well as those of a vast audience in India and throughout the world that followed the dramatic march in the newspapers. The most common item imaginable — salt — had galvanized the conscience of the nation.

On April 5, after twenty-four days, they reached the sea. The marchers had set out to break the law by the simple act of scooping up seawater and evaporating it to form crystals of salt. They spent the night before their arrival in prayer. Then, at 6:30 a.m., Gandhi stepped into the water and dipped his hand into the ocean, then picked up some salt left on the beach. The cumulative effect was electrifying.

Everywhere, people followed his example. Congress Party members took part in acts of civil disobedience, producing salt in evaporating pans on roofs and selling it. The British authorities reacted sternly, arresting sixty thousand persons, including leading members of the party such as

Jawaharlal Nehru, the future prime minister of a free India. Within the month, Gandhi was jailed yet again.

But nonviolent discipline held firmly. The campaign continued, turning its focus to the heavily-guarded Dharasana Salt Works. In columns, 2,500 *satyagrahis* advanced slowly but deliberately, ignoring the orders to halt. The protestors neither retreated nor raised their hands to protect their heads and bodies as the British officers and hundreds of Indian policemen beat them with steel-tipped *lathis*. As each column fell another advanced, only to be beaten to the ground. The carnage went on for hours — and *days* — as the *satyagrahis* held to their quiet but determined nonviolence.

Louis Fischer, one of the great biographers of Gandhi, observed, "It was inevitable, after 1930, that India would some day refuse to be ruled, and, more important, that England would some day refuse to rule. When the Indians allowed themselves to be beaten with batons and rifle butts and did not cringe they showed that England was powerless and India invincible. The rest was merely a matter of time" (Fischer 1954, 103).

In 1931 Gandhi went to London to meet with government. While there he stayed at Kingsley Hall, founded by his friend Muriel

The Round Table Conference in London

As sympathy for Indian independence grew, the government convened conferences in London to consider the implications of home rule. The first Round Table Conference was a fiasco. The only Indians invited, delegates hand picked by the Viceroy, could not speak for Gandhi and the Congress Party. When the government realized that it had to invite members of the Congress Party, a second Round Table Conference was convened after Gandhi and the Congress Party leaders had been released from jail so they could attend.

In preparation for the conference, Viceroy Lord Irwin agreed to meet with Gandhi, an event that infuriated the imperial Winston Churchill who dismissed Gandhi as a "half-naked *fakir*" (a mendicant monk). Together, Gandhi and the Viceroy agreed to allow the manufacture of salt, to release prisoners and to suspend the civil disobedience campaigns. Congress representatives consented to attend the Round Table Conference in London.

Gandhi had a number of close friends in England. The Anglican priest, Charles F. Andrews — affectionately called "Charlie" — had been a close ally and confidant of Gandhi since his South Africa days. Madeline Slade, daughter of a British admiral, had been converted by Gandhi's message. She had abandoned her upper class ways, donned a *sari,* lived in an ashram and accompanied Gandhi and his party to England. Muriel Lester also came from a wealthy background but her study of the Sermon on the Mount and Leo Tolstoy's *The Kingdom of God is Within You* led her to identify with the poor of London's East End, where she founded the settlement house, Kingsley Hall. In the 1920s Indians visiting Kingsley Hall convinced Lester that she should visit Gandhi. She first visited India in 1926 where she and Gandhi became fast friends, as they shared their pacifist work and vision. He soon began to address her as "Muriel" and she called him "Bapu" (father). Members of the ashram on the banks of the Sabarmati River were amazed and delighted to meet someone like Miss Lester — a pacifist, a vegetarian, a Christian whose life was committed to voluntary poverty. Her life and actions radically countered the Indian stereotype of Christians as a warlike people who drank beer and ate beef. As a leader of the pacifist International Fellowship of Reconciliation, she fascinated people in the ashram with stories of dedicated pacifists in the West who opposed colonialism, racism and war as they followed the Jesus of the Sermon on the Mount.

Gandhi enlisted Lester in the freedom struggle. He challenged her to take the Vow of Truth, scrupulously gathering data from government officials, business leaders, leading missionaries and excise officials. On her return to England, he asked her to lecture every possible audience about the situation in colonial India. She took up this new part of her life's work with gusto, speaking throughout England at churches, universities, student and women's groups, temperance meetings, Rotary Clubs, and open-air meetings in Hyde Park.

When Gandhi was called to London, she invited him and his party to stay at Kingsley Hall. He readily accepted, preferring to live among the poor Cockneys rather than stay in government accommodations. From September 12 to December 5 he made Kingsley Hall his headquarters. Each morning, as always — no matter where he was or how late he had stayed up the night before — he rose at 3:45 for prayers. He relished his daily hour-long walks among London's poor. The children loved him, calling him "Uncle Gandy." Each day he would return to his simple rooftop quarters after the many meetings he had to attend. When invited to meet the king and queen, he was asked if his loincloth, shawl and sandals were enough clothing for such an event. With his mischievous sense of humor he replied that the king was wearing enough for the both of them! On another occasion he told a group of well-dressed Londoners, "You people wear plus-fours; mine are minus fours" (Fischer 1954, 105). When asked why he rode third class on the trains, he replied that he did so because there wasn't a fourth class! Throughout his life he could find much to laugh about; he once remarked, "If I had no sense of humor, I should long ago have committed suicide" (*Young India,* August 18, 1921; in Gandhi 1960, 156).

Arrangements were made for Gandhi to give a half hour radio broadcast from Kingsley Hall to America. After Lester had introduced him, he appealed directly to his trans-Atlantic audience:

> In my opinion, the Indian Conference bears in its consequence not only upon India but upon the world. India is by itself almost a continent. It con-

tains one-fifth of the human race. It represents one of the most ancient civilizations. It has traditions handed down from ten thousands of years, some of which to the astonishment of the world remain intact. No doubt the ravages of time have affected the purity of that civilization, as they have that of many other cultures and many institutions.

If India is to perpetuate the glory of her ancient past it can only do so when it attains freedom. The reason for the struggle which has drawn the attention of the world does not lie in the fact that we Indians are fighting for our liberty, but in the fact that the means adopted by us have not been adopted by any other people of whom we have any record. The means adopted are not violence, not bloodshed, not diplomacy as one understands it nowadays, but they are purely and simply truth and nonviolence. No wonder that the attention of the world is directed towards this attempt to lead a successful, bloodless revolution. Hitherto nations have fought in the manner of the brute. They have wreaked vengeance upon those whom they have considered to be their enemies.

We find in searching national anthems adopted by great nations that they contain imprecations upon the so-called enemy. They have vowed destruction and have not hesitated to take the name of God and seek Divine assistance for the destruction of the enemy. We in India have reversed the process. . . .

I personally would wait, if need be, for ages rather than seek to attain the freedom of my

country through bloody means. I feel in the inner-
most recesses of my heart, after a political experience extending over an unbroken period of close
upon thirty-five years, that the world is sick unto
death of blood-spilling. It is seeking a way out,
and I flatter myself with the belief that perhaps it
will be the privilege of the ancient land of India to
show that way out to the hungering world.

After referring to the effort to rid India of untouchability
and of "the curse of drug and drink" — the latter a source of
enormous revenue for the Empire, he turned his remarks to
the needs of his people, whom he described as the
semi-starved millions scattered throughout the 700,000
villages dotted over a surface 1,900 miles long and 1,500
miles broad. It is a painful phenomenon that these simple
villagers, through no fault of their own, have nearly six
months of the year idle upon their hands.

The time was not very long ago when every village
was self-sufficient in regard to the two primary
human wants, food and clothing. Unfortunately
for us, the East India Company, by means which I
would prefer not to describe, destroyed that sup-
plementary village industry; and the millions of
spinners who had become famous through the
cunning of their deft fingers for drawing the finest
thread, such as has never yet been drawn by modern machinery, these village spinners found
themselves one fine morning with their noble oc-
cupation gone. From that day forward India has
become progressively poor.

No matter what may be said to the contrary, it
is an historical fact that before the advent of the
East India Company, these villagers were not idle,

and he who wants may see today that these villages are idle. It therefore required no great effort or learning to know that these villagers must starve in that they cannot work for six months in the year. May I not then, on behalf of these semi-starved millions, appeal to the conscience of the world, to come to the rescue of a people dying in the attempt to regain its liberty? (Lester 1932, 45–50)

In such manner, Gandhi reached the hearts of those he addressed as well as the common folk of Bow in London's East End. But what about the cotton mill workers in Lancashire who produced the cloth shipped to India? Efforts to revive spinning in the villages and the boycott of foreign cloth in India were creating layoffs and hardship in England. Despite fears that the workers would assault him, Gandhi wanted to go to Lancashire. He went anyway and won them over by revealing to them the situation in his country from the perspective of Indian villagers. He treated his adversaries with goodwill and respect, defusing their anger and evoking their empathy for the Indian workers affected so adversely by colonial policies.

In one sense the Round Table Conference was a disappointment because the British government did not budge in its refusal to relinquish the crown jewel of the empire. But Gandhi sensed that the real Round Table Conference had consisted in the multitude of friendships he had made, the sympathy he had evoked through the many speeches he had delivered, and the strength he brought to the anti-imperialist cause in England. Upon his return home he reported, "I am not conscious of a single experience throughout my three months in England and Europe that made me feel that after all East is East and West is West. On the contrary, I have been convinced more than ever that human nature is much the same, no matter under what clime it flourishes, and that if you approached people with trust and affection, you would have ten-fold trust and thousand-fold affection returned to you" (Fischer 1954, 107).

The Curse of Untouchability

After months in England and stops in Europe, he returned home. A week after he landed in India he was back in prison.

The new British government of the Conservative Party that had taken office took a decidedly sterner approach to India than had Lord Irwin and the Labor Party. Under Emergency Powers Ordinances, the Congress Party was accused of seeking to establish a parallel government. Key Congress leaders such as Nehru had been imprisoned, and Gandhi joined them upon his return.

In Yeravda prison Gandhi followed penal regulations along with his own rigorous discipline. He wrote continuously, producing over one hundred letters a week just to the members of the ashram. Since prison stationery was paid for with tax revenue he used the edges of newspapers and other paper as much as possible (Shridharani 1939, 231). While at Yeravda he learned that the British government was planning to establish a separate electorate for the untouchables — as the British called them, "The Depressed

Classes." They had already established separate Hindu and Muslim electorates so that members of each religious group could vote only for members of their own religion. Now untouchables were added, further undermining the possibility of unity that nationhood could bring.

Knowing that the nation needed new opportunities for unity, not separation, he refused to stand by while a law made permanent the separation of the nation as Hindu, Muslim and Untouchable. His concern went far deeper than the political arrangements for voting and representation. He wanted untouchability removed, root and branch. Such a serious issue provoked Gandhi to declare a fast unto death. He was willing to die to end untouchability.

All over India what came to be called the Epic Fast began to transform Hindu/*Harijan* relations. Women and women's organizations took a strong lead. From the first day of the fast, Orthodox Hindu temples that had been closed for *thousands* of years to untouchables began opening their doors. *Harijans* were allowed to use village wells and Brahmins shared benches and even meals with those whose very shadows had been considered unclean.

But dealing with deeply held prejudices and intricate political negotiations takes time — and time was running out. As the fast progressed, Gandhi quickly weakened. Representatives of the parties involved, the untouchables — the *Harijans* — the Hindus, and the government, struggled to come to an agreement, pushed by the spectre of Gandhi's worsening condition. By the fifth day doctors warned that it might be his last.

On the sixth day, in the light of the amazing changes that swept across Mother India and with the signing of an agreement he approved of, Gandhi ended his fast by sipping a glass of orange juice. His brush with death was forestalled. Louis Fischer (1954) observed, "The 'Epic Fast' improved

Harijan conditions permanently and snapped a chain that stretched back into antiquity and had enslaved tens of millions" (123).

Mohandas Gandhi truly was the Mahatma — the Great Soul — whose political genius was rooted in an authentic spirituality that made him willing to risk his own life on behalf of those whom society ignored or abused.

He knew the change in relations between Hindu and *Harijan* had to be nurtured carefully. To replace *Young India*, which had served its purpose, he started another weekly newspaper, called *Harijan*. Upon his release from Yerevda prison he spent nearly a year traveling throughout India, focusing on ending untouchability.

Constructive Program

Many recognize only one part of Gandhi's message — his call for nonviolent resistance. In doing so, however, they miss the richness and depth of his holistic philosophy that touches every dimension of life. Congress Party leader Rajendra Prasad has observed,

> There was hardly any political, social, religious, agrarian, labour, industrial or other problem which did not come under his purview and with which he did not deal in his own way within the framework of the principles which he held to be basic and fundamental. . . .
>
> If ever there was a person who took a total view of life and who devoted himself to the service of humanity, it was certainly Gandhiji. If his pattern of thinking was sustained by faith and the lofty ideals of service, his actions and actual teachings were always influenced by considerations at once moral and eminently practical. Throughout his career as a public leader extending over nearly

sixty long years, he never allowed exigencies to shape his views. In other words, he never allowed himself to use wrong means to attain the right end. (*CWMG* 1:v-vi)

Gandhi did not spend his life solely striving to end British rule; he worked to build a nation fit for nationhood. To this end he called for a constructive program in which citizens would live *satyagraha* every day, not just through individual practice but in community. He established ashrams in South Africa and India as experiments in Truth. After leading the Sabarmati Ashram near Ahmedabad for fifteen years, he decided to turn it over to *Harijans* and to start anew. He moved not to some cool hill station but rather to the poorest and hottest part of India, where no one could mistake his identification with the poor.

In 1936 he moved to the tiny, poor village of Wardha in the state of Maharashtra where he established the model village of Sevagram ("village of service") as a demonstration of social uplift through popular education, spinning, nutritious diet, and public health. Sevagram had no place for untouchability, poverty, oppression of women or child marriage. For Gandhi, democracy in India centered in the villages, which he saw as "a healthier and far more humane way of development than industrialization and urbanization with their attendant dislocation and pollution" (Easwaran 1997, 129). On January 9, 1937, he wrote in *Harijan*:

> An ideal Indian village will be so constructed as to lend itself to perfect sanitation. It will have cottages with sufficient light and ventilation built of material obtainable within a radius of five miles of it. The cottages will have courtyards enabling householders to plant vegetables for domestic use

and to house their cattle. The village lanes and streets will be free of all avoidable dust. It will have wells according to its needs and accessible to all. It will have houses of worship for all, also a common meeting place, a village common for grazing its cattle, a cooperative dairy, primary and secondary schools, in which industrial education will be the central fact, and it will have *panchayats* (village councils of five persons elected by the people) for settling disputes. It will produce its own grains, vegetables and fruit, and its own (homespun material). This is roughly my idea of a model village. . . . Given cooperation among the people, almost the whole of the program other than model cottages can be worked out at an expenditure within the means of the villagers without government assistance. (Fischer 1962, 295–97)

At another time, he referred to his goal for India in these words: "The Constructive Program is the truthful and nonviolent way of winning *Poorna Swaraj* [complete independence]" (Fischer 1962, 298).

World War II

Gandhi continued his steady efforts for Indian independence, combining challenges to British rule with constructive programs and the removal of Indian impediments to a healthy and nonviolent society, such as untouchability, child marriage, and communal conflict. In this massive undertaking, he felt called again and again to fast as a public summons to penance and purification. Gandhi's quarrel was with the British Empire and its policies, not with the worldwide tensions that simmered through the 1930s.

But developments between India and the British Raj were taking place in a world moving towards the Second World War. These overarching forces had a strong impact also on India. The threat from the fascist powers did not alter the relationship between Britain and the crown jewel of its Empire. Imperial Britain ruled as empires do. As war loomed, therefore, Gandhi was not about to let the empire make unilateral decisions that would drag India into battle without being consulted.

Gandhi saw the need to resist totalitarian tyranny, but through nonviolent means. The means he advocated for individuals as well as the entire country to pursue freedom he likewise advocated for dealing with the threat of war. He wrote, "There have been cataclysmic changes in the world. Do I still adhere to my faith in truth and nonviolence? Has not the atom bomb exploded that faith? Not only has it not done so but it has clearly demonstrated to me that the twins constitute the mightiest force in the world. Before it the atom bomb is of no effect. The two opposing forces are wholly different in kind, the one moral and spiritual, the other physical and material. The one is infinitely superior to the other which by its very nature has an end. The force of the spirit is ever progressive and endless. Its full expression makes it unconquerable in the world" (*Harijan,* February 10, 1946; in Gandhi 1949, 94). Earlier in his life, in South Africa and during World War I, Gandhi was willing to support armed conflict. He saw war as a duty for loyal citizens. But over time, especially after he witnessed the cruel and vicious British treatment of Zulus in South Africa, he changed. He answered those who charged him with inconsistency, "My aim is not to be consistent with my previous statements on a given question, but to be consistent with the truth as it may present itself to me at a given moment. The result is that I have grown from truth to truth. . . . My words and deeds are dictated by prevailing conditions. There has been a gradual evolution in my environment and I react to it as a *Satyagrahi*" (*CWMG* 90:v).

By the 1930s he had developed unconditional opposition to war. He felt that he could not declare a moratorium on his principles, no matter how evil the opponent. Evil cannot destroy evil. Fire will not put out fire. For these reasons, at the eve of World War II (February 6, 1939), Gandhi proclaimed, "My faith is brightest in the midst of impenetrable darkness" (Fischer 1954, 343).

He said that India should be prepared to resist warfare nonviolently. Should the Japanese invade from Burma, for example, the people should refuse to cooperate in any way, as invading armies depend upon collaboration. With planning, Indians could deny the Japanese such support. Noncooperation on a massive scale would baffle and undermine the invaders' plans. Though Indians would be killed, Gandhi believed fewer would die than in violent resistance and that nonviolence would leave fewer long-range consequences.

The Congress Party did not share Gandhi's pacifism, however. The Party was willing to support Britain if India was offered self-rule, but Britain was not prepared to make such an exchange. Winston Churchill, prime minister from 1940 to 1945, showed contempt for opponents of the Empire. He was as determined to hold on to British power as Gandhi was determined to bring about India's freedom. Although Churchill fiercely resisted Indian independence, in the end he failed. After the Allies won the war, the British people ousted Churchill and voted in the Labor Party, which favored India's independence.

But that is getting ahead of the story. In August of 1942 the Congress Party passed a "Quit India" resolution and asked Gandhi to lead a limited campaign of civil disobedience. Even though the action was confined to specific areas, many thousands were arrested, with volunteers filling in the places of those troops took away. Gandhi's campaign made it unmistakably clear to Britain that India was determined to become independent, war or no war.

Unwilling to countenance any disloyalty during wartime, Britain responded with force. Leaders of the Congress Party, including Gandhi and his wife Kasturbai, were arrested and imprisoned. Even Londoner Muriel Lester, on a speaking tour in Latin America, was arrested by the

British authorities in Trinidad and imprisoned for her pacifist message.

Imprisoning Indian leaders in the Aga Khan palace at
Yeravda proved tragic. One of Gandhi's aides and dearest
friends, Mahadev Desai, died of a sudden heart attack.
With Gandhi and the Congress leadership unable to exercise leadership, violence and unrest spread across India.
The government blamed Gandhi. He responded to the false
accusation with a 21-day fast. Imprisoned, unable to make
any public appeals, he felt the fast was the only way of
appeal open to him. It took his toll as he became danger-
ously weak. He survived but then in late 1943 Kasturbai,
74, turned gravely ill. In February Ba — or "mother" as she
was affectionately called — died, her head resting in her
beloved's lap. She was cremated the following day, her
ashes buried in the prison grounds next to those of
Mahadev Desai.

Mohandas and Kasturbai had been married for sixty-two
years. Referring to her as his "better half" he said "I cannot
imagine life without Ba. . . . Her passing has left a vacuum
which can never be filled" (Fischer 1954, 394). With his
health deteriorating seriously in the months following her
death, the government decided to release him. On May 3,
1944 he and his colleagues were freed from what would be
his last imprisonment. During his lifetime, he had spent
2,338 days in jail — just short of six years.

Throughout World War II, Gandhi made clear his total
opposition to war. He condemned the atomic bombings of
Hiroshima and Nagasaki and the subsequent nuclear arms
race, particularly because of the magnitude of violence they
represented. On July 1, 1946, he said:

> So far as I can see, the atomic bomb has dead-
> ened the finest feeling that has sustained

humanity for ages. There used to be the so-called laws of war, which made it tolerable. Now we know the naked truth. War knows no law except that of might.

The atom bomb brought an empty victory to the Allied arms, but it resulted for the time being in destroying Japan. What has happened to the soul of the destroying nation is yet too early to see.

Forces of nature act in a mysterious manner. We can but solve the mystery by deducing the unknown result from the known results of similar events. Slaveholders cannot hold slaves without putting themselves or their deputy in the cage holding the slave. Let no one run away with the idea that I wish to put in a defense of Japan's misdeeds in pursuance of Japan's unworthy ambition. The difference was only one of degree. I assume that Japan's greed was more unworthy. But the greater unworthiness conferred no right on the less unworthy of destroying without mercy men, women, and children of Japan in a particular area.

The moral to be legitimately drawn from the supreme tragedy of the bomb is that it will not be destroyed by counter-bombs, even as violence cannot be by counter-violence. Humanity has to get out of violence only through nonviolence. Hatred can be overcome only by love. Counter-hatred only increases the surface as well as the depth of hatred. (*Harijan,* July 7, 1946; in Gandhi 1971, 102–03)

Less than a year before he was assassinated, Gandhi wrote, "In this age of the atom bomb unadulterated nonviolence is the only force that can confound all the attacks of violence put together" (*Harijan*, November 16, 1947; in Gandhi 1971, 103). The continued faith that nations place in weapons of mass destruction confirms Gandhi's wisdom. America's Gandhi, Martin Luther King, Jr., echoed this same faith when he said, "We still have a choice today: nonviolent coexistence or violent co-annihilation. This may be mankind's last chance to choose between chaos and community" (M. L. King 1968, 223).

The Final Struggle

After a period of rest and healing following his release from prison, the Mahatma plunged into work once again. He first requested a meeting with the new Viceroy, but Lord Wavell refused to see him. Subsequently, he called for meetings with Mohammed Ali Jinnah, the fiery, aristocratic president of the Moslem League. Gandhi felt that their combined requests would prove far more powerful and persuasive with the Viceroy than either one alone. Their frustrating meetings, however, produced no positive results.

Dramatic external events, however, intervened. In 1945, first Germany surrendered, then Japan; the war ended. The Labor Party won the national elections in England and quickly moved for India's independence, taking steps to establish a federal constitution that included Congress and the Moslem League.

Jinnah, however, remained adamant: he opposed the arrangement, demanding nothing less than an independent Muslim Pakistan cut off from Hindu India. Gandhi was appalled at what he called "the vivisection" of Mother

India. Rather than healing the communal and religious differences of the subcontinent, partition would create two sovereign states. No matter how the vivisection would be carried out, Hindu and Muslim populations had become so intermixed that forced division would produce a lethal brew. Jinnah was not a devout Muslim — he drank alcohol, ate pork and married outside his faith — but he demanded a religious state. Ironically, the devout Hindu Gandhi held that India should remain strictly secular so that all religions — not just Hindu and Muslim — would be free to practice their faith and tolerate those with those who honored other traditions. The haughty and determined Jinnah played upon Muslim fears that they would become an island in a sea of Hinduism. In a Muslim state of their own, Jinnah and the Muslims could dominate a Hindu minority.

Britain's Labor government considered Jinnah's proposal, but in the end rejected it as impractical because the Muslim areas proposed by Jinnah would comprise a West Pakistan and an East Pakistan, separated by over seven hundred miles. The two sections of Pakistan would include millions of Hindus and India would contain twenty million Muslims. It would set the stage for potential fears and violence. On May 16, 1946 the British advanced their own proposal for a united India with a federal government.

Britain asked both Congress Party and the League to propose candidates. Jinnah refused to participate, so in August the Viceroy asked Nehru to form a government. Nehru visited Jinnah to offer him his choice of a cabinet position. Although Gandhi suggested prime minister or defense minister, Jinnah rejected the offers. Nehru, whom Gandhi favored as his successor, was named prime minister; he promptly appointed a qualified and diverse cabinet.

Jinnah called for a day of direct action and instructed his followers to display black flags. The subsequent riots and killings broke the hearts of all who had worked so long for *swaraj* in Mother India.

Gandhiji summoned every shred of his energy to staunch the violent hysteria that threatened to engulf the country. Hindus murdered Muslims and Muslims murdered Hindus. Forced conversions required that people adopt ways foreign to their upbringing: Hindus were made to slaughter cows and eat meat; Muslims were forced to eat pork. Despite such horrors, Gandhi brought to the public eye many cases of people who, at the risk of their lives, provided shelter and help for threatened members of the other religion. In the province of Bengal, the site of particularly loathsome fighting, Gandhi rose at 4:00 a.m. each day and walked bare-footed from village to village, staying for several days in each, talking and praying with the people and subsisting on their meager provisions of food. This continued from November 7, 1946 to March 2, 1947. Gandhi, now 78, was physically frail yet determined. He had always believed that "strength does not come from physical capacity. It comes from an indomitable will" (*Young India*, August 11, 1920; in Gandhi 1960, 96). Muslims and Hindus, at times joined by untouchables and Christians as well, came to prayer meetings at which the Mahatma appealed to their common humanity. He repeated the effort in Bihar. Everywhere he went, people came to receive *darshan*, the special blessing that comes from a holy person or sacred place.

Nevertheless, a kind of collective madness spread across the land, overwhelming Gandhi's efforts as well as those of the Congress Party and of Britain to establish a unified, independent India. Lord Mountbatten — great-great-grandson of Queen Victoria — was appointed the empire's last Viceroy and given the task of getting Britain out of India by June 1948. With Jinnah threatening civil war and violence spreading, Congress and Mountbatten wavered, then reluctantly agreed to partition as a last gasp at averting chaos.

Chaos descended nonetheless. Homes and stores were burned; hundreds of thousands died. Upwards of fifteen million fled their towns and villages in panic, hoping to find safety among their own kind in predominantly Hindu or Muslim areas. Stunningly beautiful Kashmir, claimed by both India and Pakistan, became a battle zone that has continued even to the present. Like a voice crying in the wilderness, Gandhi held out for decency, goodness and the common humanity they all shared. Gandhi feared that his life's work was coming to "an inglorious end" (Fischer 1950, 473).

On August 15, 1947, India became independent, but the Mahatma refused to join the celebrations. Instead, he fasted and prayed. Even though he was hailed as the father of the nation, he refused to visit the capital in New Delhi. Long-anticipated independence had torn Mother India apart. He saw his place instead in Calcutta, proud city of the state of Bengal. The partition of Bengal (as well as the Punjab) required in the establishment of Pakistan had unleashed months of communal violence.

Gandhi moved into the old mansion of a Muslim widow, located in a slum, where he joined the chief minister of Bengal, a peace-loving Muslim. The two men — Hindu and Muslim — appealed for calm, walking the streets and alleyways together. They demonstrated the religious unity that had always been at the heart of Gandhi's message.

On the night of August 31, crazed Hindus carrying the body of a fellow Hindu they claimed had been wounded by Muslims broke into the house where Gandhi was staying, threatening his life. Muslims encircled him to protect him until the police arrived.

The next day Gandhiji announced the beginning of a fast unto death, hoping to soften the hearts of the embattled populace. Muslims, Hindus, and Christians pledged their commitment to peace. Hundreds of on-duty policemen joined in a 24-hour sympathy fast. Tough gang leaders along with merchants and workers came to weep in the presence of their dying Mahatma, piling their discarded weapons in a heap. Once again, he had succeeded. By September 4, Calcutta was calm.

Convinced of the genuineness of their commitment, after seventy-three hours, Gandhi broke his fast. Earlier, Gandhi had written, "Fasting unto death is the last and most potent weapon in the armory of *satygraha*" (*CWMG* 75:145). With Calcutta at peace, he went to visit rioting villages and desperate refugee camps around Delhi. He refused armed guards, protecting himself only with the message of love and peace on his lips. As did the fearless Jawaharlal Nehru, he rushed to a surrounded and threatened Muslim school, to set an example of brave tolerance for the students and faculty. Gandhiji even went to a paramilitary camp of fierce anti-Muslim Hindus, telling them that the violent intolerance they advocated would kill Hinduism.

At his prayer meetings, he read the Koran to predominantly Hindu worshipers. He never tired of pleading for unity: "We must forget that we are Hindus or Sikhs or Muslims or Parsis . . . we must be only Indians. It is of no consequence by what name we call God in our homes. In the work of the nation, all Indians of all faiths are one. . . . We are Indians and we must lay down our lives in protecting Hindus, Muslims, Parsis, Sikhs and all others" (*CWMG* 90:303–04).

He loved the hymn of Cardinal John Henry Newman, "Lead Kindly Light":

> Lead, kindly Light, amid the encircling gloom,
> Lead Thou me on;
> The night is dark and I am far from home,
> Lead Thou me on;
> Keep Thou my feet, I do not ask to see
> The distant scene; one step enough for me.

He refused to retreat from the struggle. Though grief-stricken at the violence sweeping over Mother India, he steadfastly continued his tireless, brave efforts for peace. In the midst of this madness, one refugee urged that Gandhi retire to the safety of the Himalayas. Gandhi laughed heartily, saying that there he could become a double Mahatma with great crowds of people. "But what he wanted was not vainglory or ease but such comfort and strength as he could extract out of the prevailing darkness and misery" (*Harijan*, February 2, 1948; in *CWMG* 90:534).

And Gandhiji never cased to stress the central importance of what he called the constructive program — spinning, basic education, a healthy diet, natural cures, village uplift. He admonished representatives of this work to continue it without fail. The future India would emerge from healthy, self-reliant and prosperous villages. *Satyagraha* was the path for developing the national character and democratic institutions (*CWMG* 90:215–23).

"He Ram" — "Oh God"

Sensing the continued potential for uncontrolled violence, Gandhiji once again decided to heal communal animosity through fasting. Furthermore, India had reneged on its pledge of 550 million rupees for the new state of Pakistan. Gandhi felt that a failure to fulfill his duty of honor would further poison Hindu-Muslim relations.

He thus began a fast on January 13, 1948 at the Birla mansion in Delhi. Saying that he was in God's hands, he offered his fasting and prayer as an appeal to the conscience of all. His doctors worried as his fragile condition declined rapidly. Though physically weak, his spirit remained strong. He was appealing to the heart of India to follow the higher path of nonviolence, of Truth. Concern for the Mahatma's life gripped the subcontinent. At prayer meetings Muslims beseeched Allah for his life and persons of all other faith groups also prayed according to their traditions. In Delhi, shops and schools closed; petitions circulated begging Gandhiji to give up his fast. Representative delegations came to his bedside with pledges of peace and unity but until the pledges represented all groups, he vowed to continue his fast.

Finally, on January 18, after days of intensive meetings convened by Rajendra Prasad, newly elected head of the Congress Party, a large delegation of Hindu, Muslim, Jewish, Sikh, Christian, Indian and Pakistani officials came to the failing Mahatma's bedside. They pledged the safety of Muslims and the continued efforts of Hindus and Muslims to work together for the benefit of all.

Convinced that their pledges were genuine, he announced that he was breaking his fast. After reading scriptures from different traditions, including the Hindu verse "Lead me from untruth to truth,/ From darkness to light,/ From death to immortality," Gandhi and the delegation sang a Hindu hymn, followed by his favorite Christian hymn, "When I Survey the Wondrous Cross":

> See, from his head, his hands, his feet,
> Sorrow and love flow mingled down!
> Did e'er such love and sorrow meet
> Or thorns compose so rich a crown?
> Were the whole realm of nature mine,
> That were a present far too small;
> Love so amazing, so divine,
> Demands my soul, my life, my all.

Afterwards he sipped a glass of orange juice slowly. Gandhi felt joyous, deeply hopeful of amity across the land, peace between the two nations and peoples. He spoke of his long-held wish to live to 125 years. "Find in your sufferings" he admonished those crowded around him, "the seeds of a more noble victory" (Fischer 1954, 501–02).

He continued daily prayer meetings at the Birla mansion, even after a crude bomb thrown at him missed its mark. The assailant told the police of his rage at Gandhi's solicitude toward Muslims even after Hindus had been killed. Gandhi's fast had had a cleansing effect on the multitudes, but it "roused the resentment of a few fanatics who promptly put out the light that hurt their eyes" (*CWMG* 90:xiii).

Gandhiji wrote to a friend, "I am a servant of Rama. I will do this work so long as He wills . . . if I have been sincere in my pursuit of truth, nonviolence, non-stealing, brahmacharya. . . . I shall certainly be granted the kind of death that I seek . . . that should someone kill me I may have no anger against the killer . . . and I may die with Ramanama on my lips" (*CWMG* 90:489).

Another Hindu extremist stepped up to fill the place of the arrested bomb thrower. Determined to end Gandhi's life, N. V. Godse carried a hidden pistol to the Birla mansion. On the afternoon of January 30, the Mahatma came out on the grounds for the usual prayers. As hundreds crowded around, Godse moved in and, after bowing to Gandhi, fired three shots at close range into his chest. As Gandhiji fell to the ground, he called out as he died, *"He Ram"* ("Oh God"). It was 5:17 p.m.

In a broadcast to the nation a grief-stricken Nehru announced, "The light has gone out of our lives and there is darkness everywhere." Nevertheless, he predicted that in a thousand years that light would still be visible. As Nehru wrote later, "He died as he had lived, a bright star of hope and achievement" (*CWMG* 1:ix).

Mahatma Gandhi was dead. His life and message live on.

THE ASHEVILLE TIMES

STATE EDITION

Friday, January 30, 1948

GANDHI IS SHOT, KILLED BY HINDU; WILD RIOTS BREAK OUT IN BOMBAY

MAHATMA, VENERATED LEADER OF 400,000,000 IS SLAIN AS HE WALKS TO EVENING PRAYER; ASSASSINATION MAY SET ALL OF INDIA ABLAZE

Police Arrest Slayer, One Of Hindus Whom Wizened Spiritual Chief Had Led To Independence; Trouble On Subcontinent Breaks Minutes After News Is Flashed To Teeming Metropolis.

BOMBAY, Jan. 30—(UP)—

NEW DELHI, Jan. 30—(AP)—

RUSSIA CHARGES U.S. VIOLATION OF ITALIAN PACT

Ambassador Sends Protest Note Over U.S. Warships In Mediterranean.

WEEK'S SECOND CHARGE

Only Yesterday Reds Complained Over Proposed Reopening Of Air Base.

Schenck Quits Post As Associate Judge Of N.C. High Court

MICHAEL SCHENCK

TRUMAN'S PLEA FOR FULL AID IS BRUSHED OFF

Senate Leaders Ignore President's All-Or-None Appeal For Europe.

29 ARE MISSING IN PLANE LOST OVER ATLANTIC

Sir Arthur Coningham, Allied Tactical Air Head, Among Those On Board.

400 MILES FROM ISLE

Ten American Superforts Scour Region In Search Of Tudor.

Gandhi's Enduring Significance

Gandhi wanted no monuments built in his honor. He even asked that his writings be cremated with him. "My life is my message," he said (*Harijan*, June 15, 1945; in Mary King 1999, 228). He thought that the legacy of his way of life would endure, a life dedicated to experimenting with Truth. God is Truth. Truth is God. His complete commitment to this grand experiment conveys a message as timeless today as when he first said those words.

Mahatma Gandhi's appeal extends far beyond the boundaries of Hinduism. In his lifetime, he made particular efforts to reach out to the Muslims. He knew that poisonous Hindu-Muslim rivalry had to give way to the higher loyalty of their common humanity and the fact that, in their finest and deepest sense, all religions are one.

A contemporary of Gandhi, one who unfortunately has been overlooked, took this message totally to heart — Abdul Ghaffar Khan (1890–1984), a gifted, charismatic leader from the Northwest Frontier where the Khyber Pass leads through high mountain ranges into Afghanistan.

He and Gandhi could not have been more different. He was a towering, muscular 6'4" leader of the warlike Pathan tribe, who often fought to defend their honor. Nevertheless, Abdul Ghaffar Kahn recognized in Gandhi's appeals the same basic message he found in Islam. The greatest virtue was not honor, as his people had held, but compassion, for that is the nature of God. "The Holy Prophet Mohammed," said Khan, "came into this world and taught us: 'That man is a Muslim who never hurts anyone by word or deed, but who works for the benefit and happiness of God's creatures.' Belief in God is to love one's fellow men" (Easwaran 1985, 55). This belief led Khan to raise a nonviolent army to join the struggle for independence from the British. The Pathan army resisted the British forces sent against them as nonviolently as any Gandhian force could have. Strictly disciplined, willing to die rather than kill or surrender, the red-clad peace army from the Northwest Frontier formed an indispensable alliance with Gandhi. When not waging *satyagraha* they were working in their villages on constructive programs such as literacy and health education and sanitation. Abdul Ghaffar Khan became known as the Frontier Gandhi. Living into his nineties, often imprisoned by his native Pakistan, he was nominated for the Nobel Peace Prize in recognition of his lifetime of nonviolent work and witness.

Gandhi has also exercised profound influence within the civil rights movement in the United States. During his lifetime, prominent African Americans like Mordecai Johnson, president of Howard University, and Howard Thurman, well-known author and preacher, went to India to meet with Gandhi and to learn from him. In 1935 Gandhi told Thurman that African-Americans, with a powerful spirituality forged in the crucible of suffering and struggle, could deliver the undiluted message of nonviolence to humanity.

In the seminary, Martin Luther King, Jr., heard Mordecai Johnson preach on Gandhi. Hearing the story of Gandhi was "profound and electrifying" said King. He immediately purchased six books on Gandhi and began to study him intensely. As King would write later in his essay "Pilgrimage to Nonviolence," in Gandhi he found the method to apply the love ethic of Jesus to resist evil and to change society (M. L. King 1958, 94–99). Jesus' Sermon on the Mount had profoundly influenced Gandhi. Now Mohandas Gandhi had profoundly influenced Martin Luther King in following the social philosophy of Jesus. As Gandhi combined *satyagraha* with constructive programs, King joined the force of love with the creation of "the Beloved Community." Both prophets combined non- cooperation with evil with cooperation with good, a transformational approach that, as King said, would "inject a new dimension of love into the veins of our civilization" (M. L. King, 1958, 63).

Like Gandhi, King stressed inter-religious harmony. In his last book, *Where Do We Go from Here? Chaos or Community?* King describes love as "the key which unlocks the door which leads to ultimate reality . . . that force which all the great religions have seen as the supreme unifying principle" (223). He called it "the Hindu-Muslim-Christian-Jewish-Buddhist belief" found in 1 John 4:7, 8, 12: "Let us love one another, for love is of God, and everyone that loves is born of God, and knows God. He who does not love does not know God for God is love. . . . If we love one another, God abides in us and God's love is perfected in us."

Although an assassin cut short Dr. King's life at 39, there are remarkable parallels between his life and Gandhi's. They refused to demonize their enemies; they stressed the inter-relatedness of means and ends; they believed that the suffering of the innocent is redemptive. As both reached the end of their lives, although buffeted by the unrest and violence around them, the intensity of their commitment burned ever brighter. Ultimately, men of violence used gunfire to snuff out the lives of both of these prophets of nonviolence.

The imprint of Gandhi has had enormous impact on projects for advancing social justice in the United States, including the ending of segregation, the peace and environmental movement, the movement against nuclear energy, the women's movement, the movements for the rights of farm workers and movements to recognize the rights of other minorities. In the new millennium, the Gandhian heritage has motivated the anti-corporate globalization movement as well as many other people's movements. As part of this endeavor, the Albert Einstein Institution has fostered both the theoretical and applied study of the politics of nonviolent action and is working with a number of government institutions to achieve social transformation through nonviolent means.

Gandhi's constructive program lives on in the emphasis on simple living, natural foods and medicines, organic farming, and the construction of self-sustaining communities. For many involved in these projects for personal and social transformation, prayer, meditation and interfaith collaboration are indispensable resources.

Gandhi's call for a *Shanti Sena*, a peace army, is still a powerful influence in humanity's search for an alternative to war. The United Nations and many non-governmental organizations have experimented with unarmed peacemaking. The international Global Peaceforce, founded in 2002 in India, is the latest of a number of efforts to intervene nonviolently in areas of conflict and oppression.

In the half century since Gandhi's death, powerful movements of nonviolent action for liberation have grown exponentially, including diverse movements like People Power

in the Philippines, the Velvet Revolution in Czechoslova-
kia, Solidarity in Poland, the anti-apartheid movement in
South Africa, the first Intifada in Palestine, the student-led
overthrow of Milosovic in Serbia, and the peaceful overthrow of dictatorships in much of Latin America[1]

Jonathan Schell's groundbreaking *Unconquerable World:
Power, Nonviolence and the Will of the People* shows the con-
trast between coercive power and cooperative (i.e., nonviolent) power throughout history. Notwithstanding
humanity's fascination with violence that has left us with
the possibility of global catastrophe, across the world effective cooperative endeavors have widened and deepened.
Gandhi believed in "the infinite possibilities of universal
love" (Gandhi 1956, 197). Early in his career he wrote,
"Things undreamt of are daily being seen, the impossible is
ever becoming possible. We are constantly being aston-
ished these days at the amazing discoveries in the field of
violence. But I maintain that far more undreamt of and
seemingly impossible discoveries will be made in the field of
nonviolence" (*Harijan*, August 25, 1940; in Gandhi 1960,
80).

Gandhiji has left a legacy to all of us: a vibrant faith, and a
determination to experiment with Truth in every area of
life, thereby fulfilling our divine potential.

1. See Richard Deats' "The Global Spread of Nonviolence," in *Peace is the
Way*, Walter Wink, editor (Maryknoll, NY: Orbis Press, 2000)
283–95.

Selected Writings

These passages are but a tiny selection from the massive writings of Mahatma Gandhi. The Government of India has provided an enormous service by compiling the writings of Gandhi in 95 large volumes. There are also many books of Gandhi's writings on specific subjects, a number of which I bought on trips to India and from which I quote in this book. In addition, I have a number of favorite passages that appeared in the two newspapers that Gandhi edited, *Young India* and *Harijan*. Some of these passages are lacking the volume from which they originally came. Consider such quotes a personal supplement to the rest of the book; they are not intended to provide authoritative sources for researchers.

My dear Muriel,

Just to ask you to be with me in spirit to sustain me during the forthcoming ordeal. This will be in your hands after I am more than half through. That does not matter when spirit speaks to spirit. Then it is a question of asking and receiving in the same breath.

My love to you all

Bapu

$\frac{5}{8}$ 33

Letter of Gandhi to Muriel Lester

Self Awareness

The purpose of life is undoubtedly to know oneself. We cannot do it unless we learn to identify ourselves with all that lives. The sum-total of that life is God. The instrument of this knowledge is boundless, selfless service.

Letter to Muriel Lester, June 21, 1932
in Mahadev Desai, *The Diary of Mahadev Desai*, 184

This is enough for the person who is true to himself. Do not undertake anything beyond your capacity and at the same time do not harbor the wish to do less than you can. One who takes up tasks beyond his powers is proud and attached, on the other hand one who does less than he can is a thief. If we keep a time-table we can save ourselves from this last-mentioned sin indulged in even unconsciously.

Letter to Narandas Gandhi, July 10, 1932,
in *Diary*, 221

I am not at all concerned with appearing to be consistent. In my search after Truth I have discarded many ideas and learnt many new things. When anyone finds two writings of mine, do use the latter of the two on the same subject.

Harijan, April 23, 1933

No matter how insignificant the thing you have to do, do it as well as you can, give it as much of your care and attention as you would give to the thing you regard as most important. For it will be by those small things that you shall be judged.

Harijan, July 27, 1935

My imperfections and failures are as much a blessing from God as my successes and my talents. . . . Why should he have chosen me, an imperfect instrument, for such a mighty experiment? I think He deliberately did so. He had to serve the poor dumb ignorant millions. A perfect person might have been their despair. When they found that one with their failings was marching on towards *Ahimsa* (the practice of love) they too had confidence in their own capacity.

Harijan, July 21, 1940

A person often becomes what he believes himself to be. If I keep on saying to myself that I *cannot* do a certain thing, it is possible that I may end by really becoming incapable of doing it. On the contrary, if I have the belief that I *can* do it, I shall surely acquire the capacity to do it, even if I may not have it at the beginning.

Harijan, September 1, 1940

It has always been my experience that I am always true from my point of view, and am often wrong from the point of view of my honest critics. I know that we are both right from our respective points of view. And this knowledge saves me from attributing motives to my opponents or critics. The seven blind men who gave seven different descriptions of the elephant were all right from their respective points of view, and wrong from the point of view of one another, and right and wrong from the point of view of the man who knew the elephant. I very much like this doctrine of the manyness of reality. It is this doctrine that has taught me to judge a Muslim from his own standpoint and a Christian from his. Formerly I used to resent the ignorance of my opponents. Today I can love them because I am gifted with the eye to see myself as others see me and vice versa. I want to take the whole world in the embrace of my love.

Young India, January 21, 1926

I do not want my house to be walled on all sides and my windows to be stuffed. I want the cultures of all the lands to be blown about my house as freely as possible. But I refuse to live in other people's houses as an interloper, a beggar or a slave.

Inscription at the Gandhi Monument
in Washington, D.C., across the street
from the Embassy of India

Prayer and Fasting

A genuine fast cleanses body, mind and soul. It crucifies the flesh and to that extent sets the soul free. A sincere prayer can work wonders. It is an intense longing of the soul for its even greater purity. Purity thus gained when it is utilized for a noble purpose becomes a prayer. Fasting and prayer therefore are a most powerful process of purification, and that which purifies necessarily enables us the better to do our duty and to attain our goal. If therefore fasting and prayer seem at times not to answer, it is not because there is nothing in them but because the right spirit is not behind them.

Young India, March 24, 1920

[A person] is always indulgent to the body. . . . In order to counteract the indulgence, [one] should take less food than what he would think was enough [with] the likelihood of his taking what in fact was enough. So what we often think is spare or meager is likely even to be more than enough. More people are weak through over-feeding or wrong feeding than through underfeeding. It is wonderful, if we chose the right diet, what an extraordinarily small quantity would suffice.

Bapu's Letters to Mira (1949), 254;
in M.K. Gandhi, *My Religion* (Ahmedabad:
Navajivan Publishing House, 1955), 88

Prayer is the very soul and essence of religion, and, therefore, prayer must be the very core of life . . . for no one can live without religion.

Young India, January 23, 1930

[Our] destined purpose is to conquer old habits, to overcome evil . . . and to restore good to its rightful place. If religion does not teach us how to achieve this conquest, it teaches us nothing.

Young India, December 20, 1928

We are born to serve our fellowmen, and we cannot properly do so unless we are wide awake. There is an eternal struggle raging in man's breast between the powers of darkness and of light, and he who has not the sheet-anchor of prayer to reply upon will be a victim to the powers of darkness. The person of prayer will be at peace with himself and with the whole world; the person who goes about the affairs of the world without a prayerful heart will be miserable and will make the world also miserable. Apart therefore from its bearing on our condition after death, prayer has incalculable value for us in this world of the living. Prayer is the only means of bringing about orderliness and peace and repose in our daily acts.

Begin therefore your day with prayer, and make it so soulful that it may remain with you until the evening. Close the day with prayer so that you may have a peaceful night free from dreams and nightmares. Do not worry about the form of prayer. Let it be any form, it should be such as can put us into communion with the divine. Only, whatever be the form, let not the spirit wander while the words of prayer run on out of your mouth.

You, whose mission in life is service of your fellowmen, will go to pieces if you do not impose on yourselves some sort of discipline, and prayer is necessary spiritual discipline. It is discipline and restraint that separates us from the brute. If we will be persons walking with our heads erect and not walking on all fours, let us understand and put ourselves under voluntary discipline and restraint.

Young India, January 23, 1930

Silence is part of the spiritual discipline of a votary of Truth.

M.K. Gandhi, *An Autobiography, or The Story of My Experiments With Truth* (Ahmedabad: Navajivan Publishing House, 1956), 84

Nonviolence

The force of love . . . truly comes into play only when it meets with the causes of hatred. True nonviolence does not ignore or blind itself to the causes of hatred, but in spite of the knowledge of their existence, operates upon the person setting those causes in motion. . . . The law of nonviolence — returning good for evil, loving one's enemy — involves a knowledge of the blemishes of the "enemy." Hence do the Scriptures say . . . forgiveness is an attribute of the brave.

Young India, September 29, 1927

Suffering in one's own person is . . . the essence of nonviolence and is the chosen substitute for violence to others. It is not because I value life low that I can countenance with joy thousands voluntarily losing their lives for Satyagraha, but because I know that it results in the long run in the least loss of life, and what is more it ennobles those who lose their lives.

Young India, October 8, 1925

They say "means are after all (just) means." I would say "means are everything." As the means, so the end. Violent means will give violent *swaraj*. . . . There is no wall of separation between means and end. . . . I have been endeavoring to keep the country to means that are purely peaceful and legitimate.

Young India, July 17, 1924

Truth is my God. Nonviolence is the means of realizing God.

Young India, July 17, 1924

I am not a "statesman in the garb of a saint." But since Truth is the highest wisdom, sometimes my acts appear to be consistent with the highest statesmanship. But I hope I have no policy in me save the policy of Truth and Nonviolence.

Young India, January 20, 1927

There is no principle worth the name if it is not wholly good. I swear by nonviolence because I know that it alone conduces to the highest good of humanity, not merely in the next world, but in this also. I object to violence, because, when it appears to do good, the good is only temporary, the evil it does is permanent.

Young India, May 21, 1925

How are we to train individuals or communities in this difficult art?

There is no royal road, except through living the creed in your life which must be a living sermon. Of course, the expression in one's own life presupposes great study, tremendous perseverance, and thorough cleansing of one's self of all the impurities. If for mastering of the physical sciences you have to devote a whole lifetime, how many lifetimes may be needed for mastering the greatest spiritual force that humanity has known? But why worry even if it means several lifetimes? For, if this is the only permanent thing in life, if this is the only thing that counts, then whatever effort you bestow on mastering it is well spent. Seek ye first the Kingdom of Heaven and everything else shall be added to you. The Kingdom of Heaven is *ahimsa*.

Harijan, March 14, 1936

If we turn our eyes to the time of which history has any record down to our own time, we shall find that man has been steadily progressing towards *ahimsa*. Our remote ancestors were cannibals. Then came a time when they were fed up with cannibalism and they began to live on chase. Next came a stage when man was ashamed of leading the life of a wandering hunter. He therefore took to agriculture and depended principally on mother earth for his food. Thus from being a nomad he settled down to civilized stable life, founded villages and towns, and from member of a family he became member of a community and a nation. All these are signs of progressive *ahimsa* and diminishing *himsa*. Had it been otherwise, the human species should have been extinct by now, even as many of the lower species has disappeared.

Prophets and *avatars* have also taught the lesson of *ahimsa* more or less. Not one of them has professed to teach *himsa*. And how should it be otherwise? *Himsa* does not need to be taught. Man as animal is violent, but as Spirit is nonviolent. The moment he awakes to the Spirit within, he cannot remain violent. Either he progresses toward *ahimsa* or rushes to his doom. That is why the prophets and *avatars* have taught the lesson of truth, harmony, brotherhood, justice, etc. — all attributes of *ahimsa*.

Harijan August 11, 1940, in M.K. Gandhi, *All Men Are Brothers*, compiled and edited by Krishna Kripalani (New York: Continuum, 1980), 79

Having flung aside the sword, there is nothing except the cup of love which I can offer to those who oppose me. It is by offering that cup that I expect to draw them close to me.

Young India, February 4, 1931, in *My Religion*, 58

It is easy enough to be friendly to one's friends. But to befriend the one who regards himself as your enemy, is the quintessence of true religion.

Harijan, May 11, 1947, in *My Religion*, 58

It is no nonviolence if we merely love those that love us. It is nonviolence only when we love those that hate us.

From a private letter, December 31, 1934, in *My Religion*, 58

The weak can never forgive. Forgiveness is the attribute of the strong.

Young India, April 2, 1931, in *My Religion*, 59

Amritsar has become a place of pilgrimage not only for me but for every Indian. No penance will suffice for the evil that has been wrought by our hand in Amritsar. It is true that a large number of our people were killed in Jallianwala Bagh. But we ought to have maintained peace even if everyone present had been killed. It is not right, in my opinion, to take blood for blood. Our religion teaches us not to inflict pain on anyone.

Speech delivered to the women's meeting, Amristar, November 4, 1919, in *The Collected Works of Mahatma Gandhi* (hereafter referred to as *CWMG*), 16:286

I have been asked whether the brother or other relatives of the late Rajabali should demand compensation from the Government for his murder. The deceased himself would not have considered such a death a loss. He would have held that such a murder, if allowed to go unavenged, would ultimately put an end to further murders and was therefore beneficial. To demand even the smallest compensation for the death of such a man is bound to wash away to some extent the good that it might do. How can the spirit of the deceased tolerate this? I find much substance in this argument. Murder cannot be avenged by accepting compensation for it. The proper way to avenge murder is not to answer murder with murder. Those who hold this view will not demand money for murder or commit murder in retaliation. Avenging murder with murder will only lead to an increase in murders. We can see it clearly today. It may satisfy the individual but I am certain that is can never bring peace to society or advance it. The question can certainly arise what an individual can do in a society where murder for murder is the rule. The answer would lie not in precept but in setting an example. And only those have a right to set an example who have the right to avenge, namely, the relatives of Rajabali. In the end the decision has to be theirs. I have only pointed out the way of *ahimsa* as I have understood it.

Sevagram, August 9, 1946 [From Gujarati]
Harijanbandhu, August 18, 1946, in *CWMG*, 85:140

What I am just now combating is the position that is taken up by some of the finest writers in Europe, and by some of the finest writers even in India: that man, as a class, will never be able to arrive at a stage when he can do without retaliation. I have a fundamental quarrel with that position. On the contrary, I say that man, as man, will not realize his full destiny, and his full dignity, until he has been so far educated as to be able to refrain from retaliation. Whether we like it or whether we do not like it, we are being driven to it. It would be to our credit if, instead of being driven to the position, we will take ourselves to it, and I have come this evening to ask you to exercise this privilege, the privilege of voluntarily taking up this idea in practice. Indeed, I ought not to have to be speaking to a Christian audience on this, because some of my friends tell me that I am really a Christian when I talk about non-retaliation. Little do they know that I have got to strive with the Christians as I have to with Hindus and my Muslim friends. I do not know many Christians who have adopted this thing as a rule of their life. Some of the very best Christians that I know do not admit that this is the teaching of Christ. I do believe that it is the teaching of Christ. They say it was meant merely for his twelve disciples, not meant for the world, and they quote some passages from the New Testament in support of their contention.

Speech delivered to a meeting of Christians;
Calcutta, August 4, 1925, in *CWMG*, 28, 22

I have found that life persists in the midst of destruction and therefore there must be a higher law than that of destruction. Only under that law would a well-ordered society be intelligible and life worth living. And if that is the law of life, we have to work it out in daily life. Whenever there are jars, whenever you are confronted with an opponent conquer him with love — In this crude manner I have worked it out in my life. That does not mean that all my difficulties are solved. Only I have found that this law of love has answered as the law of destruction has never done. The more I work at this law, the more I feel delight in life, delight in the scheme of this universe. It gives me a peace and a meaning of the mysteries of nature that I have no power to describe.

Young India, October 1, 1921, in *My Religion,* 62

Poverty and Hunger

A starving man thinks first of satisfying his hunger before anything else. He will sell his liberty and all for the sake of getting a morsel of food. Such is the position of millions of the people of India. For them liberty, God and all such words are merely letters put together without the slightest meaning.... If we want to give these people a sense of freedom we shall have to provide them with work which they can easily do in their desolate homes and which would give them at least the barest living.

Young India, March 18, 1926

I am endeavoring to see God through service of humanity, for I know God is neither in heaven nor down below, but in everyone.

Young India, August 4, 1927

We should be ashamed of resting or having a square meal so long as there is one able-bodied man and woman without work or food.

All Men Are Brothers, 172

The economic constitution of India and for that matter of the world should be such that no one under it should suffer from want of food and clothing.... Everybody should be able to get sufficient work to enable him to make the two ends meet. And this ideal can be universally realized only if the means of production of the elementary necessaries of life remain in the control of the masses. These should be freely available to all as God's air and water are or ought to be, they should not be made a vehicle of traffic for the exploitation of others. Their monopolization by any country, nation or group of persons would be unjust. The neglect of this simple principle is the cause of the destitution we witness today not only in this unhappy land but in other parts of the world, too.

All Men Are Brothers, 166

The saving of labour of the individual should be the object, and honest humanitarian consideration, and not greed, the motive. Replace greed by love and everything will come out right.

Young India, November 13, 1924

I will give you a talisman. Whenever you are in doubt, or when the self becomes too much with you, apply the following test.

Recall the face of the poorest and weakest person whom you have seen, and ask yourself if the next step you contemplate is going to be of any use to that person. Will that person gain anything by it? Will it restore that person to a control over his or her own life and destiny? In other words, will it lead to *Swaraj* (independence) for the hungry and spiritually starving millions? Then you will find your doubts and your self melting away.

R.K. Prabhu, This Was Bapu (1954),
in My Religion, 52

That economics is untrue which ignores or disregards moral values. The extension of the law of nonviolence in the

domain of economics means nothing less than the introduction of moral values as a factor to be considered in regu-
lating international commerce.

All Men are Brothers, 166

The World's Seven Blunders

Politics without Principles
Wealth without Work
Commerce without Morality
Education without Character
Pleasure without Conscience
Science without Humanity
Worship without Sacrifice

Gandhi's grandson, Arun Gandhi, told me
that he learned this from his grandfather.
The words are found at the
tomb of the Mahatma

Women

If I were born a woman, I would rise in rebellion against any pretension on the part of man that woman is born to be his plaything. I have mentally become a woman in order to steal into her heart. I could not steal into my wife's heart until I decided to treat her differently than I used to do, and so I restored to her all her rights by dispossessing myself of all my so-called rights as her husband.

The Mind of Mahatma Gandhi, compiled by
R.K. Probhu and U.R. Rao (London:
Oxford University Press 1945), 111

Of all the evils for which man has made himself responsible, none is so degrading, so shocking or so brutal as his abuse of the better half of humanity — to me, the female sex, not the weaker sex. It is the nobler of the two, for it is even today the embodiment of sacrifice, silent suffering, humility, faith and knowledge.

The Mind of Mahatma Gandhi, 112

To call woman the weaker sex is a libel; it is man's injustice to woman. If by strength is meant brute strength, then, indeed, is woman less brute than man. If by strength is meant moral power, then woman is immeasurably man's superior. Has she not greater intuition, is she not more self-sacrificing, has she not greater powers of endurance, has she not greater courage? Without her, man could not be. If nonviolence is the law of our being, the future is with woman. . . . Who can make a more effective appeal to the heart than woman?

The Mind of Mahatma Gandhi, 112

If only women will forget that they belong to the weaker sex, I have no doubt that they can do infinitely more than men against war. Answer for yourselves what your great soldiers and generals would do, if their wives and daughters and mothers refused to countenance their participation in militarism in any shape or form.

M.K. Gandhi, *Women and Social Injustice* (Ahmedabad: Navajivan Publishing House, 1954), 18

On War and the Atomic Bomb

I did not move a muscle when I heard that the atom bomb had wiped out Hiroshima. On the contrary, I said to myself, "Unless now the world adopts nonviolence, it will spell certain suicide for humanity."

Harijan, September 29, 1946

The two opposing forces are wholly different in kind, the one moral and spiritual, the other physical and material. The one is infinitely superior to the other which by its very nature has an end. The force of the spirit is ever progressive and endless. Its full expression makes it unconquerable in the world.

Harijan, February 10, 1946

Nonviolence is like radium in its action. An infinitesimal quantity of it embedded in a malignant growth acts continuously, silently and ceaselessly till it has transformed the whole mass of the diseased tissue into a healthy one. Similarly even a little of true nonviolence acts in a silent, subtle, unseen way and leavens the whole society.

Harijan, November 12, 1938

Has not the atom bomb proved the futility of all violence?

Harijan, March 10, 1946

I hold that those who invented the atom bomb have committed the gravest sin in the world of science. The only weapon that can save the world is nonviolence. Considering the trend of the world, I might appear a fool to everyone. But I do not feel sorry for it. I rather consider it a great blessing that God did not make me capable of inventing the atomic bomb.

Biharmi Komi Agman, April 25, 1947,
in *CWMG,* 87:255

So far as I can see, the atomic bomb has deadened the finest feeling that has sustained humanity for ages. There used to be the so-called laws of war, which made it tolerable. Now we know the naked truth. War knows no law except that of might.

The atom bomb brought an empty victory to the Allied arms, but it resulted for the time being in destroying Japan. What has happened to the soul of the destroying nation is yet too early to see.

Forces of nature act in a mysterious manner. We can but solve the mystery by deducing the unknown result from the known results of similar events. Slaveholders cannot hold slaves without putting themselves or their deputy in the cage holding the slave. Let no one run away with the idea that I wish to put a defense of Japan's misdeeds in pursuance of Japan's unworthy ambition. The difference was only one of degree. I assume that Japan's greed was more unworthy. But the greater unworthiness conferred no right on the less unworthy of destroying without mercy men, women, and children of Japan in a particular area.

The moral to be legitimately drawn from the supreme tragedy of the bomb is that it will not be destroyed by counter-bombs, even as violence cannot be by counter-violence. Humanity has to get rid of violence only through nonviolence. Hatred can be overcome only by love.

Harijan, July 7, 1946, in *CWMG,* 84:394

This feeling of helplessness in us has really arisen from our deliberate dismissal of God from our common affairs. We have become atheists for all practical purposes. And therefore we believe that in the long run we must rely upon physical force for our protection. In the face of physical danger we cast all our philosophy to the winds. Our daily life is a negation of God.

Young India, May 25, 1921

It is open to the great powers to take up nonviolence any day and cover themselves with glory and earn the eternal gratitude of posterity. If they or any of them can shed the fear of destruction, if they disarm themselves, they will automatically help the rest to regain their sanity. But then these great powers have to give up imperialistic ambitions and exploitation of the so-called uncivilized or semi-civilized nations of the earth and revise their mode of life. It means a complete revolution. Great nations can hardly be expected in the ordinary course to move spontaneously in a direction the reverse of the one they have followed and, according to their notion of value, from victory to victory. But miracles have happened before and may happen in this very prosaic age. Who can dare limit God's power of undoing wrong? One thing is certain. If the mad race for armaments continues, it is bound to result in a slaughter such as has never occurred in history. If there is a victor left, the very victory will be a living death for the nation that emerges victorious. There is no escape from the impending doom save through a bold and unconditional acceptance of the nonviolent method with all its glorious implications.

Harijan, November 12, 1938

Nonviolence is the only antidote to the atom bomb. Truth and nonviolence are more powerful than the atom bomb. A nation or group which has made nonviolence its policy cannot be subjected to slavery even by the atom bomb.

Harijan, August, 8, 1946, in *CWMG*, 85:133

There is no hope for the aching world except through the narrow and straight path of nonviolence. Millions like me may fail to prove the truth in their own lives, that would be their failure, never that of the eternal law.

Harijan, June 29, 1946

Glossary

Ahimsa	nonviolence, harmlessness
Ashram	a community set apart by a discipline and common life together
Bapu	father; a term of great respect
Bhagavad Gita	Song of the Blessed One, sacred book of Hinduism
Brahmacharya	celibacy
Dharma	duty, moral law
Harijan	"child of God," the name Gandhi gave to the outcastes, the untouchables
Khadi or Khaddar	hand-spun and hand-woven cloth
Mahatma	great soul
Mantra	a word or phrase repeated over and over
Raj	empire, e.g., the British Raj
Rishi	sage
Sarvodaya	the way of life that promotes the well-being of all
Satyagraha	truth-force, nonviolent resistance
Satyagrahi	one who practices *satyagraha*
Swadeshi	love of one's country and its indigenous products
Swaraj	self-rule, independence; *Hind Swaraj,* Indian home rule
Vedas	the earliest and most sacred Hindu writings

Chronology

1869   (October 2) Mohandas Gandhi born in Porbandar, India, the youngest son of Karamchand and Putlibai Gandhi

1883   Arranged marriage to thirteen-year-old Kasturbai Makanji

1888   (September 4) Sails to England to study law

1890   Graduates from law school

1891   Admitted to the bar and returns to India; unsuccessfully tries to begin legal career

1893   Moves to Durban, South Africa to work for Dada Abdullah & Company, an Indian Muslim firm. Seeking to travel first class, is thrown off the train, a life-changing event

1894   Organizes Indian National Congress to advocate for Indian rights

1897   Briefly returns to India, then brings wife and children to South Africa

1904   Begins first ashram, "Phoenix Farm," near Durban

1906   Leads first *satyagraha* campaign of nonviolent resistance in Transvaal

1908   First imprisonment for resisting government policy requiring Indians to register. Advocates burning registration cards

1910   Establishes second ashram, "Tolstoy Farm," near Johannesburg, after correspondence with Leo Tolstoy in Russia

1913   Leads Indian miners in march across Transvaal and is arrested

1915   Returns to India

1916   Founds Satyagraha Ashram near Ahmedabad

1919   (April 6) Calls for a national strike with prayer and fasting
(April 13) 379 innocent men, women and children shot by British soldiers in Amritsar
Becomes editor of *Young India,* English newspaper, and *Navajivan,* Gujarati newspaper

1920   Elected president of the All India Home Rule League. Mass civil disobedience grows in *satyagraha* campaigns for independence

1922   Suspends civil disobedience due to outbreak of violence. Writings in *Young India* lead to charges of sedition, resulting in six-year prison term.

1924   Released from jail due to poor health. Fasts to promote Hindu- Muslim unity. Promotes use of homespun cloth (*khadi*) and the end of untouchability.

1929   Arrested for burning foreign cloth in promotion of *khadi.*

1930   Leads 241-mile Salt March to the sea to protest British tax. Makes salt from sea water, leading to arrest and imprisonment.

1931   (August–December) Attends Round Table Conference in London; stays at Muriel Lester's Kingsley Hall in impoverished East End instead of in government quarters.

1932   (January) Arrested one week after returning to India, imprisoned without trial. Still in prison begins fast unto death to end untouchability.

1933   Launches *Harijan,* a weekly replacing *Young India.* Tours India opposing untouchability

1934   Congress Party promotes "Quit India" resolution

1935   Establishes "Sevagram," a model village in Warda.

1942   Calling for civil disobedience in midst of war, arrested with Kasturbai and imprisoned in Aga Khan Palace.

1944   Kasturbai, 74, dies in prison on February 22. Gandhi, in poor health, released on May 6 — last time to be imprisoned. Holds talks with the Muslim League's leader, Jinnah for Muslim-Hindu cooperation.

1947   Walks in strife-torn Bihar. Meets with Jinnah, and Lord Mountbatten. On August 15 India is partitioned from Pakistan and both are granted independence. Gandhi adamantly opposes partition. Visits strife-torn regions, fasts and prays in Calcutta. After three days of fast unto death, rioting ceases.

1948   (January 30) At age 79, shot and killed by Hindu extremist in Delhi at the Birla House during a prayer meeting. Final words are "Oh God, Oh God" (*He Ram, He Ram*).

Bibliography

Books by Mohandas Gandhi

The Collected Works of Mahatma Gandhi. New Delhi: The Publications Division, Ministry of Information and Broadcasting, Government of India., 1958–1992. Citations from *The Collected Works* in this book list volume number and date.

Gandhi, Mohandas K. *All Men Are Brothers.* Compiled and edited by Krishna Kripalani. Ahmedabad: Navajivan Publishing House, 1960.

_____. *An Autobiography or The Story of My Experiments With Truth.* Ahmedabad: Navajivan Publishing House, 1956.

_____. *For Pacifists.* Ahmedabad: Navajivan Publishing House,1971.

_____. *Hind Swaraj or Indian Home Rule.* Ahmedabad: Navajivan Publishing House, 1962.

_____. *My Religion.* Ahmedabad: Navajivan Publishing House, 1955.

_____.*The Message of Jesus Christ.* Bombay: Bharatiya Vidya Bhavan, 1986.

_____. *Non-Violence in Peace & War*, Vol. II. Ahmedabad: Navajivan Publishing House, 1949.

_____. "Non-Violence — The Greatest Force." *The World Tomorrow* (October 5, 1926): 143.

_____. *The Science of Satyagraha*. *Bombay*: Bharatiya Vidya Bhavan, 1970.

Other Books Referenced in this Study

Easwaran, Eknath. *Gandhi The Man: The Story of His Transformation*. Tomales, CA.: Nilgiri Press, 1997.

_____. *A Man To Match His Mountains. Badshah Khan, Nonviolent Soldier of Islam*. Petaluma, CA: Nilgiri Press, 1985.

Fischer, Louis. *Gandhi: His Life and Message for the World*. New York: Signet Key Book, New American Library, 1954.

_____, editor. *The Essential Gandhi*. New York: Random House, 1962.

Jones, E. Stanley. *Mahatma Gandhi. An Interpretation*. Nashville: Abingdon Press, 1948.

King, Jr., Martin Luther. *Stride Toward Freedom*. New York: Harper & Row, 1958.

_____. *Where Do We Go From Here: Chaos or Community?* New York: Harper & Row, 1968.

King, Mary. *Mahatma Gandhi and Martin Luther King, Jr:. The Power of Nonviolent Action*. Paris: UNESCO, 1999.

Lester, Muriel. *Entertaining Gandhi*. London: Ivor Nicholson & Watson, 1932.

Nehru, Jawaharlal. *Toward Freedom: The Autobiography of Jawaharlal Nehru*. New York: John Day,1941.

Shridharani, Krishnalal. *War Without Violence*. New York: Harcourt, Brace And Company, Inc., 1939.